Lewis Wright

The Brahma Fowl

A Monograph. Third Edition

Lewis Wright

The Brahma Fowl
A Monograph. Third Edition

ISBN/EAN: 9783337124076

Printed in Europe, USA, Canada, Australia, Japan

Cover: Foto ©Andreas Hilbeck / pixelio.de

More available books at **www.hansebooks.com**

MR. L. WRIGHT'S DARK BRAHMA COCKEREL.

"FAVORITE 3."

1ST AND CUP AT CRYSTAL PALACE, AND 1ST AND EXTRA SPECIAL £10 PRIZE
FOR BEST BRAHMA COCKEREL AT BIRMINGHAM, 1872.

THE

BRAHMA FOWL:

A MONOGRAPH.

BY

LEWIS WRIGHT,

AUTHOR OF " THE PRACTICAL POULTRY-KEEPER," THE " ILLUSTRATED
BOOK OF POULTRY," &c., &c.

THIRD AND REVISED EDITION.

LONDON :
CASSELL, PETTER, AND GALPIN, LUDGATE HILL ;
AND
" JOURNAL OF HORTICULTURE AND COTTAGE GARDENER"
OFFICE, 171, FLEET STREET.

1873.

PRINTED BY
J. WRIGHT AND CO., STEPHEN STREET,
BRISTOL.

PREFACE TO THIRD EDITION.

AS was stated in the first edition of this little work, it was not written merely from a poultry - fancier's enthusiasm. We had, it is true, grown fond of the *Brahmas;* we had found there was much to learn about them, and much character in them. But we had also come to the conclusion—right or wrong—that it was a *good* fowl; that though not perfect by any means, it was upon the whole perhaps the best adapted to the English climate, and occupied among the races of poultry a position similar to that of the Shorthorn among the races of cattle; that as a purveyor of good, honest, *solid food*—though we do not say of the very choicest—it was what Miss Watts once called it, "about the best fowl we have ever had."

Finding then, that the breed was often misunderstood, and its very merits converted thereby into defects, while on the other hand perhaps no variety was more difficult than the Dark Brahma to breed to an exhibition standard, we thought it worth while to write a book "about nothing but Brahmas." We trusted thereby, as we said, to give some assistance to the fancier ; but we hoped also to increase somewhat the resources of the farmer, to add to the luxuries of the breakfast-table, and far—far more—to cheapen wholesome food in these hard times for some striving middle-class families.

We succeeded. We had no reason to expect pecuniary return, and we did not expect any, from a work appealing only to the cultivation of one among the many breeds of poultry : but to our utter astonishment a second edition was called for in less than eighteen months ; and the second having "mysteriously disappeared" in about the same space of time, demands the present carefully revised edition. We also received from our many readers such earnest requests for a correspondingly full treatment of the *whole* subject of poultry, as led to the projection of a general work* upon a scale never before even attempted. Most gratifying of all, however, while the entries of Brahmas at all leading shows have more than doubled, the general standard of perfection has been so raised, that birds which would have certainly won when this work was first written would now stand no chance whatever.

This last fact has not been forgotten in preparing the

---

* The Illustrated Book of Poultry : with 50 Colored Plates.

present edition. While the groundwork remains the same, every care has been taken to bring the directions for breeding up to the best standards of the present day, and with especial reference both to the black breast in Dark cocks now so generally demanded, and the beautiful blue grey in the pullets which we have personally striven so hard to restore. We have, as before, told *all we know* upon the subject : if anything material be omitted, it arises not from jealousy, but from "ignorance, sir, sheer ignorance." With poor Artemus Ward, we can't say fairer than that.

We feel pleasure in repeating the expression of our obligation to others, whose names are mentioned in these pages, and especially to Mr. Teebay and Mr. F. Wragg, from whom much of our earliest and soundest knowledge of the Brahma has been derived. As regards ourselves, cut off as we were at the time this work was first written, by a very small town yard, from most of the honors of exhibition, we felt it then necessary almost to apologise for what might have appeared presumption in professing to treat of the breed at all. Though want of time still prevents our exhibiting on more than one or two occasions during the year, such an apology is probably not now needed ; but if it is, the statement that, besides the few birds we have been able to show personally, a large proportion of the winning chickens of the last two or three seasons have been bred on one side or the other from our own strain, and that a hen hatched from eggs supplied by us* has realised the highest price given for a single hen of *any* breed during the last twenty years, may perhaps be considered a pardonable vanity. We make it solely as stated, in justification of " The Brahma Fowl;" the third edition of which we now commend to the same kind indulgence which has already given us so much more favourable a reception than we could either have hoped or desired.

Crouch End, London,
    August, 1873.

---

* The hen alluded to, having won the cup at Yarmouth, and been stated by the judge to be the best he had ever seen, was purchased by Mr. H. Lingwood at the extraordinary price of £20. The same breeder, from a cockerel also hatched from eggs supplied by us, bred chickens the year before, of which it was stated in a poultry periodical that eleven birds won cups or first prizes. This is by no means a solitary instance.

CONTENTS.

THE BRAHMA FOWL.

CHAPTER I.

The Origin of Brahmas.

PROBABLY no subject whatever has caused so much discussion in the poultry world as the origin of the Brahma fowl, though the variety was unquestionably first introduced into England as late as the year 1852, when two pens were shown at Birmingham by Mrs. Hosier Williams and Dr Gwynne. On the one hand it was said that the fowl was a new breed, or at least a new sub-variety with distinct characteristics, originally imported from India ; whilst on the other side it was contended that the birds were either a cross between the Cochin and Malay, or at best, if a pure race at all, with nothing but color to distinguish them from Cochins. At length the controversy died away, without the matter being really settled after all.

After so long an interval we should not have attempted to re-open the question, but that the correct decision of the matter has an important bearing upon the question of the formation of new varieties and the origin of species, and is so so quoted by Mr. Darwin. To support the doctrine of the

development or evolution of distinct varieties or species from
pre-existing species, it is of much importance to collect any
evidence which may be obtainable tending to authenticate
actual examples of this process; and though the creation of a
mere variety would not have the importance in a controversy
of more specific differences, yet could it be established that
even so peculiarly distinct a variety as the Brahma had actually
been evolved by the art of man—not gradually or in course of
time, but *suddenly* by a lucky cross—from pre-existing races
of fowls, and had been bred for more than twenty years since
without further change or deterioration, the fact would unquestionably be entitled to very great weight. It was perhaps
natural, therefore, that Mr. Darwin should have somewhat too
eagerly seized upon it, and with a carelessness which is most
strongly to be condemned in a scientific man, but which our
own knowledge of the facts of poultry-breeding enables us to
assert is paralleled by some other instances in the same work,*
stated, without any authority whatever but the bare *ipse dixit*
of Mr. Tegetmeier, that " Dark Brahmas, which are believed
by some fanciers to constitute a distinct breed, were undoubtedly formed in the United States within a recent
period by a cross between Chittagongs and Cochins." Hence
the solution of the question becomes of interest to the
naturalist, and even to the theologian ; and having entered
upon an investigation of the matter some time since from
simple interest in the breed, it appeared to us possible

---

* The Variation of Animals and Plants under Domestication ; by Charles
Darwin, M.A., F.R.S. London : 1868.

even yet to throw some additional light upon the subject, and with the aid which recent researches have afforded to point with almost certainty to a scientific and rational conclusion.

And first, to quote by far the most able exponent of the Cochin theory, Mr. Tegetmeier says,* " There is not a particle of evidence to show that they came from India. The banks of the Brahma-Pootra have long been in the possession of the British, and no such fowls were ever seen in the locality. In fact, Brahmas originated, not in India, but in America ; and the two varieties of the breed now known as Dark and Light had unquestionably *very distinct origins.*"† He then goes on to say that the Light birds "undoubtedly originated in, or were identical with, those grey fowls that from the very first came over from Shanghæ with the buff and partridge birds now universally known as Cochins," and, as undoubted evidence of this, quotes Mr. Burnham's amusing and unscrupulous work, entitled *A History of the Hen Fever*, published at Boston in 1855. In this work Mr. Burnham, who it will be remembered, sent over some of the earliest so-called Brahmas as a present to Her Majesty, which arrived in January, 1853, affirms in effect that *he originated them*, relating how, out of a hundred Cochin fowls " of all colours, grades, and proportions," brought over by an enterprising captain, he selected "a few grey birds, that were very large and consequently very fine." These he bred with other grey stock he had, and "soon had a

---

* The Poultry Book, p. 55.

† These Italics are our own, the statement being of some importance.

fine lot of birds."* We have thus two very definite statements
by Mr. Burnham : first, that *he was the founder* or original
breeder of Brahmas ; and secondly, that the Light variety
were pure, uncrossed *grey Cochins.*

On the other hand, of the Dark breed, which Mr. Tegetmeier
has already affirmed to be of " very distinct origin" from the
Light, he writes simply, " Mr. Burnham states that they were
grey Chittagongs crossed with Cochins. ' Of this,' he says, ' no
one now entertains a doubt.'" As a single line, however, by
no means does justice to the illustrious authority quoted as
decisive, we transcribe from *The Hen Fever* the entire passage.
It will at all events amuse the reader, and is also useful as
showing how far Burnham's description agrees with or differs
from that of a genuine or real Brahma.

" When, in 1850 and '51, the ' *Bother'ems*' began to be
brought into notice, I saw at once that, although this was
bubble number two, it ought to have been number *one*
decidedly.

" Never was a grosser hum perpetrated than this was,
from beginning to end, even in the notorious hum of the
hen-trade. There was absolutely nothing whatever in it,

---

* Grey Shanghæs were frequently met with, in America as well as England,
both before and after Brahmas were introduced. Mr. White, of East Randolph,
Mass., is considered by United States fanciers to have been the first who imported
this variety, and he never pretended for a moment that they were identical with
the Brahmas. Their color is more what is called in America " Dominique," or
resembling the " Dominique" fowl : and is not what we call pencilling, but almost
exactly the color and marking of the Cuckoo Dorking or Scotch Grey. In fact
they are often still shown as *Cuckoo* Cochins in England.

about it, or connected with it, that possessed the first shade of substance to recommend it, saving its *name*. And even this could not have saved it, but from the fact that nobody (not even the originator of the unpronounceable cognomen himself) was ever able to write or spell it twice in the same manner.

"The variety of fowl itself was the *Grey Chittagong*, to which allusion has already been made, and the *first* samples of which I obtained from 'Asa Rugg,' (Dr. Kerr) of Philadelphia in 1850. Of this no one now entertains a doubt. They were the identical fowl all over—size, plumage, and characteristics.*

"But my friend the Doctor wanted to put forth something that would take better than his ' Plymouth Rocks ;' and so he consulted me as to a name for a brace of *grey*

---

*As the Chittagong has been affirmed by others besides Burnham to be identical with the Brahma, it may be as well to state, what is not perhaps generally known, that Dr. Bennett was a great admirer and breeder of this fowl before he obtained his Brahma stock, and could not have failed to detect any similarity. In the American Poultry Book of 1850, he gives a detailed description of it, stating the cock to be of a *grey* color in the body, and the legs usually quite clear, but occasionally feathered, with very frequently *nine or ten toes* between them, and the comb *large and single*. No evidence could be plainer of a Dorking cross; and accordingly Dr. Kerr, another well-known breeder of the variety, who is alluded to by Burnham in this very paragraph, describes it as "a mongrel, and like all mongrels, of little real value." Both he and Geo. Smith, Esq., of Philadelphia, unite in describing the birds as "poor layers and bad sitters," very lazy, and subject to gout in the feet. These testimonies from the two gentlemen who have bred the Chittagong most extensively in America, must be of far more weight than the opinion of any in England who have *never seen the bird ;* and the assertion that a fowl possessing the qualities described, by a lucky cross originated the Brahma, makes larger demands on our credulity than almost any other theory which could be advanced.

fowls I saw in his yard. I always objected to the multiply-
ing of titles; but he insisted, and finally entered them at
our Fitchburg Depôt Show as '*Burrampooters*,' all the way
from India.

"These three fowls were bred from Asa Rugg's Grey
Chittagong cock, with a yellow Shanghæ hen, in Plymouth,
Mass. They were an evident cross, all three of them having
a top knot! But, *n'importe.* They were then "Burrampooters.'

"Subsequently these fowls came to be called 'Buram-
pootras,' 'Barram Putras,' 'Bramapooters,' 'Brahmas,' 'Brama
Puters,' 'Brama Poutras,' and at last 'Brahma Pootras.' In
the meantime, they were advertized to be exhibited at various
fairs in different parts of the country under the above changes
of title, varied in certain instances as follows : 'Burma Porters,'
'Bahama Paduas,' 'Bohemian Pudras,' 'Bahama Pudras ;' and
for these three *last* named, prizes were actually offered at a
Maryland fair in 1851 !

"Peter Snooks, Esq. it appears had the honour to be the
fortunate possessor of this invaluable variety of fancy poultry
in its unadulterated purity of blood. He furnished from his
own yard samples of this rare and desirable stock for His
Royal Highness Prince Albert, and also sent samples to
several other noted potentates, whose taste was acknowledged
to be unquestionable, including the King of Roratonga, the
Rajah of Gabblesquash, His Majesty of the Cannibal
Islands, and the Mosquito King. Peter supplies the annexed
description of the superior properties of this variety of
fowls :—

"'The '*Bother'em Pootrums*' are generally hatched from eggs. The original pair were not! *they* were sent from India, by way of Nantucket, in a whale ship.

"'They are a singularly *picture-squee* fowl from the very shell. Imagine a crate-full of lean, plucked chickens, taking leg-bail for their liberty, and persevering around Faneuil Hall at the rate of five miles an hour, and you have an idea of their extremely ornamental appearance.

"'They are remarkable for producing bone, and as remarkable for producing offal. I have had one analysed lately by a celebrated chemist with the following result—

Feathers and Offal	39·00
Bony Substances	50·00
Very tough Muscle and Sinew	9·00
Miscellaneous Residuum	2·00
	100·00

" A peculiarly well-developed faculty in this extraordinarily fine breed of domestic fowl is that of *eating*. ·A tolerably well-fed Bother'em will dispose of as much corn as a common horse,' insists Mr. S——. This goes beyond *me;* for I have found that they could be kept on the allowance, ordinarily, that I appropriated daily to the same number of good sized store hogs. As to affording them *all* they would eat, I never did that. Oh no! I am pretty well off, pecuniarily ; but not rich enough to attempt any such foolhardy experiment as that !

"But Snooks is correct about one thing. 'They are not fastidious or particular about *what* they eat.' Whatever is portable to them is adapted to their taste for devouring.   Old hats, India-rubber, boots and shoes, or stray socks are not out-of-the-way fare with them.   They are amazingly fond of corn, especially *a good deal of it.*   They *will* eat wheaten bread rather than want."

This matchless effusion was at the time considered by some to settle the question as to the origin of Brahmas.   By some it may be thought to do so still : others will wonder whether any one would like to hang a house-cat upon such evidence : for ourselves, we shall simply bring Mr. Burnham's statements, as we would any other, to the test of facts.

And first it may be well to quote the account given in *The Poultry Yard,* being a quotation from a letter written by Mr. V. Cornish, of Connecticut, U.S.   Mr. Cornish says :

" In regard to the history of these fowls very little is known. A mechanic, by the name of Chamberlain, in this city, first brought them here.   Mr. Chamberlain was acquainted with a sailor, who informed him that there were three pairs of large imported fowls in New York; and he dwelt so much upon the enormous size of these fowls, that Mr. Chamberlain furnished him with money, and directed him to go to New York and purchase a pair of them for him ; which he did at a great expense.   The sailor reported that he found one pair of light grey ones, which he purchased ; the second pair was dark-coloured ; and the third pair was red.   The man in New York, whose name I have not got, gave no account of their origin, except that they had been brought there by some sailors in the India ships.   The parties through whose hands the fowls came, as far back as I have been able to trace them, are all obscure men. I obtained my stock from the original pair brought here by Mr. Chamberlain, and have never crossed them in the least. These fowls were named Chittagong by Mr. Chamberlain, on account of their resemblance, *in some degree*, to the fowls then in the country called by that name ; but it is certain they never bred until they reached this town."

It should be remembered that this was the *first* published history of the matter ; but by advocates of the Cochin theory it was supposed to be disproved by that of Mr. Burnham, and no inquiry seems to have been made by either party as to how far either account was corroborated or confuted by other testimony ; though it will at once be seen that this is the question upon which almost everything depends. Here, therefore, we commenced our investigation ; and must in justice acknowledge our obligations to Mr. F. Crook, who has aided us by making special inquiries in America on our behalf regarding circumstances and facts now nearly forgotten, and by information obtained in reply from various correspondents afforded us assistance, the value of which, in a question of this kind, it is very difficult to estimate.*

---

* As Mr. Crook, since the publication of the former editions of this work, has alluded in some notes on Brahmas for the second edition of Mr. Tegetmeier's "Poultry Book" to information which he " has supplied as the basis for an entire work upon the subject ;" and so far as we are aware no other " work upon the subject" than the present has appeared, it may seem due to ourselves to state, that Mr. Crook has supplied no information to these pages but what is honestly acknowledged, and was not communicated with till the work was far advanced. If therefore " The Brahma Fowl" be alluded to, the reader can judge for himself the precise amount of "basis" afforded by information, which we are nevertheless glad again, and heartily, to acknowledge.

It appears then, from the statements of these private correspondents and from various papers of the period, that one of the first public appearances of the Brahmas took place at the Fitzburg Poultry Show, on October 2nd, 3rd, and 4th, 1850. They were chickens, and were the property of Dr. J. C. Bennett, of Great Falls. This pen was considered magnificent in every way, and was the principal attraction of the show. The obvious question at once occurs, from whom did Dr. Bennett procure these birds? and it is impossible to doubt his own statement, made in answer to every enquiry, that he had "purchased them, at a very high figure, from *Mr. Cornish, of Connecticut.*" A portion of Mr. Cornish's letter, not quoted in *The Poultry Yard*, states that Chamberlain brought his fowls into the State in the early part of 1846: and it will be seen that these facts and dates, though entirely independent, corroborate Mr. Cornish's account in every particular, and Mr. Burnham's general claim to have been the *first* breeder of Brahmas at once falls to the ground.

Dr. Bennett bred from this pair of chickens shown at Fitzburg, and the produce were of the first order; for in November, 1851, he again exhibited chickens of this breed, as did also Mr. Parkinson and Mr. S. O. Hatch, *all of Connecticut.* Again these Brahmas were the centre of attraction; but on this occasion Mr. Hatch beat the Doctor, who straightway purchased all of Mr. H's birds at the show. These facts also strongly, though indirectly, corroborate Mr. Cornish's account; proving on the one hand that, for at least two seasons, *Connecticut* was the head quarters of the breed; and on the other, that from the very first it bred with extreme purity as regards all the characteristics.

We also find distinct evidence as to Mr. Burnham, who, it appears, was a large professed dealer in and breeder of poultry as a matter of business. He visited the New England Society's Show in 1850, and endeavoured to purchase some of the Brahma stock there exhibited, but failed. On this occasion he *admitted*, both to Mr. Cornish, who was also there, and to Mr. Morse, the Secretary, that he had *never seen anything like them before*, and again that he "had never seen the pure Brahma-Pootras before," although he had (as we also find) been selling birds he *called* Brahmas before this, and at high prices. Amongst other testimony to the latter fact, and also to the essential difference at this date between Burnham's sham Brahmas and Dr. Bennett's genuine ones, at the same Society's (New England) Show in 1852, Dr. De Gruy stated that he had previously bought some of Mr. Burnham's so-called Light Brahmas, and they were "no more like the true Brahmas than an owl is like a hawk!" and that having just afterwards purchased a pair of Dr. Bennett's strain, for which he gave fifty dollars, "he was actually offered 150 dollars for them, which he refused!"

It appears, therefore, indisputable, that up to 1852 Mr. Burnham had no real Brahmas in his possession; but having a large number of Cochins, of all colours, that he endeavoured to *imitate* for business purposes a fowl he found so popular and valuable, at the same time being perfectly aware of the great difference between the real strain and his own. What he may have done after that date is uncertain : it is believed

that at the Boston Show in 1852 some of the real Brahmas
were purchased for him, though not in his name; and in
singular contrast to the amusing passage above quoted, we
accordingly find him writing concerning *these* birds : "the
specimens exhibited at the late fair in Boston, 1852, were
extraordinary specimens, both old and young—they are really
an *extraordinary race*, and cannot fail to become popular."

Regarding the question of personal testimony, therefore, as
between Mr. Cornish or Dr. Bennett on the one hand, and
Mr. Burnham on the other, there cannot now be two opinions.
That Burnham bred many tolerable *imitations* before he got
possession of real Brahmas, is likely enough, and the distribu-
tion of these birds has done more to complicate the whole
question than anything else ; as they have been not only bred
inter se, but crossed in all good faith with the genuine race,
so giving rise to strains of all degrees of purity and shades of
character.   Thus, the difference in shape of the Light birds
sent by him to the Queen in 1852, and the Darks sent by him
after, as shown in the cuts of *The Illustrated London News*, is
most apparent.   Mr. Tegetmeier hence argues that Dark and
Light had "very distinct origins;" but it is apparent to every
breeder of the fowl that the one variety figured (the Dark) *is
a Brahma*, while the other is not; and the inference is, that
previously to the last consignment Burnham had got hold of
the genuine strain, again exactly corroborating the testimony
above.   But there is other evidence of the same fact.   Thus,
in the *Cottage Gardener* of 1853, Mr P. Jones states the fact
of a pair of grey chickens he bought breeding *"silver cinna-
mon"* offspring; whilst the pure unmixed stock of Dr. Gwynne

(who had his direct from Dr. Bennett), Mr. Sheehan, and others, "invariably bred pure grey." Again, in December of the same year, the Editor of the same journal states, that "while what have been considered as the purest strain of the Brahma-Pootras *have thrown pure chickens only*, we know on good authority that the produce of *imported birds of equally high pretensions* have produced ·buff chickens with black hackles."

Further testimony however being still desirable, a valued American correspondent, Colonel Mason C. Weld, associate-editor of one of the most widely-circulated agricultural papers in the States, forwarded to Mr. Cornish a series of questions on the subject, and transmitted to us Mr. Cornish's reply, as follows :—

"NEW BRITAIN, CONNECTICUT, U.S.,
November, 9*th*, 1869.

" MASON C. WELD, ESQ.

"DEAR SIR,—I have your letter of 5th. I give below all the facts relating to the early history of the Brahma Pootra fowls I can call to mind at this late day. At an earlier day 'I could have given a history of these fowls more satisfactory to myself, *i.e.*, more fully than I can now ; nevertheless, so far as it goes the truth of it cannot be questioned. I will at once answer your questions.

" 1st.—Mr. Chamberlain's Christian name is Nelson H.

"2nd.—The sailor's name I never made note of, and cannot give it.

" 3rd.—The ship arrived in New York in September, 1846. The first brood came out in May, 1847. I purchased the most of that brood in August, and the old pair the April following.

"4th.—The name of the port from which the ship sailed with the fowls on board is Luckipoor. This port is up from the mouth of the Brahma-Pootra river, in India. The name of the ship I cannot give, neither can I give the name of the captain. Did not at the time think it of importance, and made no record of it.

" 5th.—The Brahmas were first exhibited in Boston by Mr. Hatch, of Hampton, Conn., under the name of Grey Chittagongs, in 1850. I declined exhibiting mine

at that time ; I believed them to be a breed different from the Chittagong, and preferred to accumulate stock and test them further before bringing them out publicly.

"6th.—I attended the exibition at Boston, and contended that they differed
from the Chittagongs, and should pass under a different name.   A committee was
appointed, and the name Brahma-Pootra given : it being the name of the great
river from the banks of which they came.   The name was then established.

"7th.—Weight of cocks, full-sized, twelve to fourteen pounds ; cocks, six to
seven months, nine to ten pounds. Hens when first introduced, nine to ten pounds.

"8th.—I did notice the 'pea-comb' on the first birds.   It was small.   It was
not so with all, and yet it appeared different from the comb of the Chittagong.

"9th.—There was no degeneracy in the birds of my breeding.   I had some
specimens larger than the imported birds.   I sold no birds until December, 1850.
I sold at first at twelve dollars per pair, and soon after from fifteen dollars to fifty
dollars per pair.   The price went up as the fowls became better known, and
recognised as a distinct breed.

"10th.—I bred them eight years, when my health failed, and I was obliged to
leave all care for a time.

"11th.—*There was a tendency to throw dark chickens*, but a greater tendency to
become lighter, and yet not white like the White Dorking.   All breeds of fowls
having dark and light feathers can be varied either way, to darker or lighter, by
choosing always the darkest or the lightest for breeders. If your stock of Brahmas
are pure, and they are allowed to breed together promiscuously, the variation in
colour will be slight. I never bred to either extreme.

"Yours truly,

"VIRGIL CORNISH."

The conflict of assertion, it will be seen, is absolute and
direct between Mr. Cornish and Burnham, but this last letter
is absolutely conclusive unless it can be discredited ; for
Burnham's own account does not claim anything on his part
till several years after the date here named as that of the
introduction into Connecticut of these fowls. It was therefore
attempted to discredit it ; and in a review by the *Field** of the

---

* It should be stated that Mr. Tegetmeier is Poultry Editor of this journal.
We should not of course mention such a fact, but that his own printed announcement of it on every possible occasion removes any delicacy on the subject.

work in which Mr. Cornish's note was first published, the
following remarks were made :—

"A sailor, whose name nobody knows, belonging to a ship whose name no one
remembers, and having a captain whose name is unknown, is stated to have sailed
from the port of Luckipoor with the original of these fowls.   It is a pity Mr.
Cornish did not also forget the name of the port ; for geographical truth compels
us to state that Luckipoor is not a port at all, but a small inland town, situated in
the Himalaya mountains, 100 miles from the nearest point of the Brahma-Pootra
river."

On reading this singular criticism, we felt somewhat puzzled
to decide whether the writer intended it as a daring speculation
upon our own and his readers' ignorance of Indian geography, or
really meant it in good faith, owing to his own.   But adopting
the latter supposition, and availing ourselves of such authorities
as were at hand, the following reply was sent; and courteously
inserted by the editor of the *Field*, with the curious comment
appended :—

"I must ask you for a few lines in reference to what you state concerning Mr.
Cornish's geographical accuracy, in stating that the birds came from Luckipoor,
'up from the mouth of the Brahma-pootra river in India.'   You state that it is a
pity Mr. Cornish 'did not forget' the port as well as the name of the ship and
captain, inasmuch as Luckipoor is 'not a port at all, but a small inland town in the
Himalaya mountains, 100 miles from the nearest point of the Brahma-Pootra river.'
This statement is so important that I am sure you will allow me to correct it.

"First, I think I may say that Mr. Cornish, had he been 'making up' a story,
would have taken the very simple precaution of seeing to it that his geography was
not so grossly inaccurate as you imply.

"But, secondly, to come to facts.   In the excellent Gazetteer published by
Messrs. Blackie, Luckipoor is described as being 'sixty miles S. by E. of Dacca,
near the left bank, and within a few miles of the mouth of the Great Megna, with
which it communicates by a small river.   The Megna has a breadth near Luckipoor
of more than ten miles.'   As the name Megna might mislead some few readers,
I add the description of this, also from Blackie : 'Megna, the name given to the
river Brahma-Pootra throughout the latter part of its course, and by which it is
known at its embouchure in the bay of Bengal.'

" So much for Blackie. I need not add, what is so well known to you, that even the ' small rivers' of India are easily navigable. But, further, in the ' Penny Cyclopædia,' art. ' Hindostan,' p. 217, is the following passage, speaking of the rise of the tide in the river Brahma-Pootra : ' At the bifurcation of the Chudna branch it rises between thirty-one and thirty-two feet ; at Dacca only fourteen feet ; and further southward, at Luckipoor, not more than six feet.'

"These are the only works of reference I have just at hand. I can easily find other testimony, but think you will allow these to be quite sufficient. I enclose for your inspection, however, a rough sketch, drawn for me from memory alone by an old officer who spent twenty years in India, and who inclosed it in a letter which had no reference to your review, or to any mistake in geography whatever. You will see his sketch exactly agrees with both the above.

" I trust you will consider the authorities here quoted as evidence sufficient that the place whose name Mr. Cornish so unfortunately did *not* forget is, at all events, geographically possible to have had the honour he assigns it of first exporting the Brahma fowl.　　　　　　　　　　　　　　　" L. WRIGHT."

[" We have communicated with our reviewer, and he replies as follows.—ED. —' Luckipoor, as appears from Indian geographies, is a name applied to more towns than one. There is a Luckipoor in the Hills, in 27 degrees N., the one referred to by me ; another in the Sunderbunds, 22 degrees N. latitude by 89 degrees E. longitude ; and a third in 22 degrees 53 minutes N. latitude by 90 degrees 53 minutes E. longitude, which appears to be the one referred to by Mr. Wright. In " Fullarton's Gazetteer," which is a more copious one than that Mr. Wright quotes, this town is said to be "a few miles inland from the east bank of the Megna," and the fact of its being situated on a small river communication therewith will not alone suffice to make the town a port, otherwise many places on the tributaries of our chief rivers would rise in rank. Certainly I do not find it among the list of ports mentioned in the Sailing Directions of British India. In reality, however, the existence or otherwise of the port will not settle the existence of the Brahma-Pootra fowl in that district—which is the real question at issue. As far as I can learn from naturalists and others acquainted with that part of the world, no such race of bird is to be found there. If it really does exist, surely there ought to be some more satisfactory evidence of the fact than has hitherto been forthcoming.' "]

Dismissing the question of Luckipoor, therefore, with the simple remark that the advocate of Burnham's tale should have looked up his Indian geography *before* finding fault with

Mr. Cornish's : and noting very briefly that it is scarcely matter for wonder the name of ship and sailor should be forgotten, since no one would have supposed more than twenty years ago that they would be so imperiously demanded ; what *is* of importance would seem to be the position and trustworthiness of Mr. Cornish ; and this we cannot show better than by quoting part of another letter to ourselves from that gentleman. The letter itself is dated New Britain, Connecticut, April 12, 1870, and we ought to add that we have verified its statements from independent sources:—

"As my name has appeared in this country and in England in connection with the history of the Brahmas, I beg you to allow me a word for myself.

"My letters to Dr. Bennett and others, from which you make extracts, were called for, written, and published at an early day, when the parties who brought them (the Brahmas) from India to New York, and from thence to Hartford, Connecticut, were *living and to be seen* by all men. They *were* often seen and inquired of by parties interested, and their statements were never discredited, nor doubted by any one except Mr. Burnham, and by him only by falsely stating that he originated them in his own yard.

"At the time the original pair of Brahmas were brought to Hartford, Connecticut, I was an officer at the Retreat for the Insane in that city ; having in charge all the business of that institution, except that which belonged strictly to the medical department. I had purchased a farm of fifty acres for the institution, and thereon fitted up a large yard for the accommodation of rare animals, flowers, and birds ; and had placed in them more than *sixty* distinct breeds (of fowls and other animals), in which I took much interest and pleasure. This I had done for the amusement of the convalescent patients. I had no pecuniary interest in bringing out the Brahma fowls, but saw at once that they were a distinct breed, and worthy of a high place."

We have already seen that Mr. Cornish's statement was published long *before* Burnham's. It gives a perfectly clear, consistent, and simple account of the origin of certain birds, which are proved by independent testimony to have been all

C.

obtained from the State of Connecticut; and the obvious
question is, by what testimony save of the clearest, best sup-
ported, and most convincing character, may such an account
be disproved ? and is Burnham's sufficient to disprove it ?
We can only reply that no one but Mr. Tegetmeier in England
ever attached to any statement of Burnham's the least
importance whatever.   Even he calls his great authority
"unscrupulous," as well he might after the unblushing account * of the motives which solely dictated the "present to
Her Most Gracious Majesty ;" and among Americans themselves his book was never received with anything but a laugh
at what was universally understood to be another attempt of
the same sort at a trading puff.   As an instance of this
general appreciation of the man, we had quite recently an
announcement from a valued American correspondent that .
"our old friend Burnham" had "let himself out again ;" and
were somewhat perplexed by the enigmatical information,
until the receipt of a copy of " Burnham's New Poultry-Book,"
published in 1871, elucidated the mystery.   This second book
was, in all respects, worthy of the first, being a series of
advertising puffs in the most approved "spread-eagle" style
from beginning to end : and it especially amused us to note
how the author had, with a most laudable regard to reciprocity,
in return for Mr. Tegetmeier's unhoped-for quotation of the

---

* It begins thus :—" Finally the idea occurred to me that a present of a few of
the choicest of these birds to the Queen of England wouldn't prove a very bad
advertisement for me in this line.   I had already reaped the full benefit accruing
from this sort of 'disinterested generosity' on my part towards certain American
notables."

former work, repaid the favour by quoting *his* as ample "authority" on the very same point ; each thus referring to the other, and to the other alone, as confirming his own views! It is the simple fact that not one American writer (and but one English) ever regarded Burnham's account as of the slightest value.

Whether the latter may have bred, amongst others, very tolerable *imitations* of Brahmas, is, as we before observed, not the question. We have seen that there were two qualities of birds known in the early days—one a spurious, which bred mongrel-progeny, and could be traced to Burnham ; the other pure, which was always traced to Connecticut, or a little later to Dr. Bennett, who procured his from that State. But such, and accounts of such published after the pure Brahmas were even publicly shown, cannot invalidate a *consistent and credible account given from the very first* of the genuine strain ; and, as Mr. Cornish justly argues, confirmed and inquired into at the time and on the spot, while all the witnesses were alive and available for examination. Burnham himself states in his last work that he was a member of *that very committee*, at Boston, which was appointed in 1850 to settle the name, as mentioned in Mr. Cornish's letter to Colonel Weld. He says that the name was thus given by them "against his protest ;" and the unavoidable conclusion from that simple fact alone must be, that parties *who knew both* considered Mr. Cornish the most reliable witness of the two.

When therefore Mr. Tegetmeier, in the face of the preceding statements and facts, most of which were accessible to him, affirms that "there is *not a particle of evidence* to show that they came from India," it is impossible to deal with such an assertion in any serious manner ; and his various objections to the purity of the breed, on examination, are found to have little more force.   First of all, we find neither testimony nor facts to corroborate the opinion that there were two races of "very distinct origin," whilst many facts prove there was but one.   We have made many enquiries relative to this matter, and all with the same result.   Miss Watts, whose strain is probably the only one now existing which has not been crossed, has assured us in the most distinct manner that she had but *one stock*, from which by selection she had bred both Dark and Light.   To put the matter more definitely still, Mr. Joseph Hinton—also one of our oldest breeders—states that his birds were originally Light, from Mr. Garbanati, Dr. Gwynne, and Mr. Davies of Hounslow.   He afterwards received a medium colored or rather dark cock from Mr. J. K. Fowler, from which bird and the darker of his Light hens, he bred a most beautiful Dark cock (second at the Crystal Palace Show) and several hens so heavily and intensely marked as to be almost black.   From these birds were bred his well-known cock *Champion*, and hens as we see them now.   Thus, by the third year, and solely by the established rules of breeding, he had *transformed his strain* from Light to Dark, obtaining also in transit several laced birds of great beauty, which it is a pity were not perpetuated.   In our own yard, we have found that black Brahmas could be easily bred if necessary, or on the other hand, that they could be brought back again to Light. Now it is incontestable that the first Brahmas were neither so dark nor so light as now.   They were always called *grey*, a term which would not describe either variety now shown. Since, then, undoubted Light strains can produce Dark, and Dark have a constant tendency, if bred carelessly, to produce Light, it is obvious that the original intermediate strain would breed either with much greater facility, and may well be the parent stock of both.

Having so far cleared the ground, we may now examine the breed itself more in detail : since even Mr. Cornish's stock might of course have been Cochins, as much as Burnham's. And here we may quote an argument of Mr. Tegetmeier's which is of decided weight. "It has been remarked," he says, "that it is a fact universally recognized by comparative anatomists, that the distinguishing characters of nearly allied varieties are more strongly marked in the bones of the skull than in any other part of the body. Now the skull of the Cochin is vaulted and arched, both from before backwards and from side to side, and possesses a peculiarly marked groove, extending from before backwards on the frontal bone; and—what every anatomist will regard as a character of great value—the long axis of the aperture through which the spinal chord issues from the skull is the perpendicular one. Now in these characters the skull of the Brahma is identical; whereas in all ordinary breeds of fowl the long axis of the occipital foramen is placed transversely, the skull wants the distinguishing frontal peculiarities, and the remarkable arched or vaulted character found in both these breeds." This argument is forcible, and strictly philosophic. In order to do full justice to it, we have had engraved the accompanying illustration, Fig. 1. representing the occipital foramen of a Cochin of the natural size, and Fig. 2. that of

the *Gallus Bankiva*, or wild type of the Game Fowl; both
being taken from Mr. Darwin.   It will be seen that not only
is the aperture much longer vertically, in proportion, in
Fig. 1. but assumes quite a triangular form, which is entirely
wanting in the foramen of the typical bird.   Here then is a
character which, if the example were unique, would be of
unquestionably very great value.   But when we come to
examine other races, Mr. Darwin himself (whose accuracy
is unimpeachable) tells us in the course of an investigation

Fig. 1.   Fig. 2.

unconnected with Brahmas altogether, that the skull of the
Dorking not unfrequently exhibits the same peculiar shape
of the foramen; that it occasionally occurs in some other
breeds ; and that in one or two varieties of Bantams the
character is almost constant.   On the whole therefore, while
the craniological resemblance between Cochins and Brahmas
must be allowed great weight, it will not do for the present to
regard it as conclusive.

Similarly, the general outline, the gigantic size, the yellow
legs feathered to the toes, the color of the eggs, the period of
laying (daily or nearly so) and the frequency of incubation, all
are points in which there is a great resemblance between the

two breeds. But here again qualification must be made. There are other fowls which lay every day; the Malay shares the resemblance in size, color of eggs, and massive yellow shanks; and the frequency of incubation on an average is much less in the Brahma than the Cochin, though both are greater than in other breeds. With regard to the latter point however, must be considered the hypothesis of a cross with the Malay, which might be expected to produce just such an effect on the reproductive organs.

In many other points, however, the differences between Brahmas and Cochins are so marked and striking, that it is strange so acute an observer as Mr. Tegetmeier should, in common with other writers, have overlooked them. In addition to the well-known pea-comb and the prominent breast, which seem to have been the only points hitherto remarked, we may draw attention to the length of the deaf-ears compared with the wattles; the location of the crop, which in Cochins is *above* and in Brahmas *below* the normal position; and the peculiar formation of the tail, which is more fully described and illustrated in Chapter III. The latter we regard as perhaps the strongest character of all.

Returning here for a moment to early personal testimony, we may remark that in the summer of 1852, before any Brahmas had arrived in England, Dr. Bennett wrote of them that they differed from Shanghæs as follows: "comb (*i.e.* when single) and wattles smaller, but ear-lobes much longer; shorter in leg and more compact (a most remarkable assertion when the alleged Malay cross is considered—see Mr. Crook's experience, page 35), deeper breasted and shorter quartered."

The voice is also a point of some value in a question of this kind. It is therefore important to note, that while the crow of both Cochin and Malay is hoarse and guttural, as is too well known by unlucky neighbours, that of the Brahma, when mature, is almost always long and clear. Still there are exceptions, and we have found either character hereditary ; so that this feature, so far as it goes, would point to a mixed origin for certain strains—a conclusion singularly corroborated by the actual evidence already reviewed.

In general habits and carriage we get on rather more definite ground, the Brahma having a distinct character of its own. It is the most active of any variety except the Game ; sprightly and alert in spite of its great size, it is up the first and goes to roost the last of all our breeds. The carriage of the cock differs greatly from that of both Malay and Cochin, being bold and free, after the style of the Game fowl, and with a decisive, vigorous, *clean* step very remarkable in so large a breed. The bird is likewise of very high courage; yet is quite devoid of ferocity, and of a very tame and sociable disposition, differing greatly from both the alleged parents of his race. In both sexes there will also be observed peculiarities in the shape and carriage of the head and wings.

Still further, we will here quote Mr. F. Crook of Forest Hill, a well-known exhibitor of Light Brahmas. Knowing this gentleman to have paid great attention to the question we are considering, and to have made many experiments in crossing with special reference to it, we requested that he would favor us with any definite conclusions he had arrived at. Respecting pure-bred Cochins he remarks :

"A great evidence against the Shanghæ origin of Brahmas is the ground-colour of the plumage. White Cochins are white-feathered down to the skin, which latter usually appears yellow : whereas in really good Light Brahmas the fluff of the feather is grey, and so abundant that the skin is with difficulty seen—when however made visible it is not yellow, but of a pinky cast. Again, the very finest single-combed birds, with many good pea-combed ones—in fact all the first birds, seen in this country, and many of the very best since, had a perceptible bar or splash of black upon the wing ; and the best single-combed birds now bred in America have it still. Now this is a point which beyond controversy never occurred in White Cochins, and is almost conclusive to one acquainted with the two breeds. Another very peculiar feature in Light Brahmas is the peculiar narrow white fringe on the feathers of the cock's tail; this is now difficult to obtain even in good strains, but in 'experimental' birds is never seen at all."

The great force of these observations can only be felt by those practically acquainted with the matter. On the point of the white edge alluded to in the upper feathers of the cock's tail, we can testify from experience that though breeders have endeavoured to banish it, the tendency yet exists even in *Dark* Brahmas, still further proving that they had a common and not a "very distinct" origin from the Light.* We have

---

* Mr. Joseph Hinton draws our attention also to the color of the legs. White Cochins have a constant tendency to bread olive-colored or green legs, which is a well-known disqualification in the show pen. Now Light Brahmas when pure bred, have *never been known* to produce a green leg, very strongly corroborating the hypothesis pressntly advanced, that they belong to the *more ancient race* of the two.

frequently bred it ourselves, and since in the earlier editions of
this work we pointed it out as rather a beauty to be cultivated,
and having no relation at all to the common blemish of "white
in the tail," it has been more common. The splendid cockerel
of Lady Gwydyr's, which won all the cups in 1871-2, possessed
this feature in perfection, both top feathers of the tail being
beautifully laced with white all round.

Respecting a cross as the possible origin of Brahmas, Mr.
Crook has transcribed from his notes the nearest results of
many attempts made by him in this direction, which as they
have never previously been published will be interesting.

"Parents, White Cochin Cock and Cuckoo Dorking hen.
Produce : large framed heavy hens, of nearly white ground,
color speckled and streaked with grey. The cocks fine form
and shape, with speckled body on white ground. Combs
single ; legs of both sexes poorly feathered, and tails much too
large. This produce however appeared to me likely to answer
the purpose ; so I mated one of the cocks again with white
Cochin hens. The produce had better feathered legs, but
were bad shape and nearly white, shanks mostly pink ; combs
single as before.

"Parents, grey Malay cock with white Cochin hens. The
produce was nearer the mark in many respects than the last
named, the pullets being queer shaped birds with white bodies,
straight tails, and lightly pencilled hackles, head neat, but bad
expression, and comb hardly visible. The cockerels had white
compact bodies, lightly pencilled hackles, tail full but *drooping*,*

---

* This to be noted, as compared with the remarkably *erect* tail of the Brahma,
much more erect than that of the Cochin.

and genuine long, flat, Malay quarters; comb coarse and warty. The best cockerel was a beautiful bird in all but what I wanted.

" Parents, Partridge Cochin cock with white Dorking hens. Produce : pullets with whitish dull grey bodies and pencilled hackles, very heavy in color.   Cocks large-framed birds with fair shape, dark grey bodies and heavy hackle ; single comb.

" I matched this last cockerel again with white Cochin hens. Produce : Cochin-like, bad-shaped, but finely framed heavy hens, of white ground color with the body feathers prettily laced, and hackles darkly pencilled. Cockerels fine heavy birds similar in color to the pullets, but rather lighter, with single combs.

" One of these last cockerels I mated again with buff Cochin hens.   Produce : large pullets, buff and brown on the back, hackles pencilled, legs well feathered, with single combs. Cocks similar, but more brownish yellow all over, with pencilled hackles and single combs. A pen of these last were sent to a show in 1864, with the notification, ' this pen is the result of many attempts to produce a Light Brahma.' No notice was taken of them in any way.

" I should add, that seeing a remark in print which much astonished me, to the effect that any two opposite varieties of fowl with single combs would produce a true triple or pea-comb, I tried the very varieties mentioned as an instance, viz., a Cochin hen with a Spanish cock; but the result with me was a perfectly arched Spanish comb of finer quality than usual."

In fact, the mere probability against a new breed of fowls being founded, by any cross *at once* breeding true to colour and feather (to say nothing of other points) is so strong,

that the theory would never have been entertained at all, were
not a few instances apparently established in which such
has been the case. Few as such instances are, we must
therefore for the present admit there is a bare possibility that
Brahmas may have formed another example of this rare
phenomenon in breeding; and proceed to consider rather more
minutely the pea-comb, which, as being so peculiar, we
might reasonably hope would assist us in arriving at the
truth, and bringing our investigation of this curious subject
to a close.

This comb is unique, differing both from the single, the
rose, the cup, and Malay comb; and while it is unquestionable
that many of the early pure Brahmas had single combs, it is
still more incontestable that the great majority had from the
first this peculiar pea-comb, which had such a superior *vitality*
or relationship to the breed, as to remain a predominant
feature in the fowl. Now it will have been noticed, that not
only did Mr. Crook's experiment of crossing Spanish with
Cochins fail to produce this comb, but the Malay cross—often
alleged as the source—failed likewise. We also know for a
fact, that scores of attempts have been made by other parties
to produce the pea-comb by a Malay cross, without effect.
These facts seem conclusive, and are often quoted as such by
those who hold to the distinctiveness of the Brahma. Yet one
indisputable exception in a case of this kind has the force of
many ; and there are several instances of the true pea-comb
entirely independent of any Brahma cross. Many years ago
a correspondent of *The Poultry Chronicle* related how he had
obtained it by crossing a Malay hen with a Cochin cock—the

reverse of Mr. Crook's experiment; and Mr. Joseph Hinton
has recorded the fact of having obtained seven or eight pea-
combed chickens in one brood, from the very cross between
Spanish and Cochin which Mr. Crook attempted in vain.   He
also states that he has observed "capital pea-combs" more
than once upon his pure-bred Malays, and yet another upon a
mongrel whose parentage could not be identified.*   In rare
instances pea-combs have been observed upon pure-bred
Cochins.   Lastly, the Sumatra game-fowl has a pea-comb
—smaller and less distinct, it is true, than that of the Brahma,
but still typical and well marked; and the so-called "Indian
game" common in Cornwall often presents beautiful specimens
of the pea-comb.

Here, then, we appear further from any definite conclusion
than ever, and at first sight it seems as if this vexed question
were to baffle every possible avenue of investigation!   But, as
is often the case, we get our clearest light where we least
expect it.   Ere we know it, we are getting on definite scientific
ground, and there are facts and principles which not only
furnish a clue to these·apparently contradictory phenomena,
but make them actual guides to the issue of our inquiry.

These principles, in some of their results, are known to all
breeders, and are seen in daily operation in the return of

---

* In a letter received since the above was in type, Mr. Hinton informs us that
the mongrel in question was a small bird of black-red game color; and also that in
April 1869, whilst on a journey, he came across another mongrel bird with a well-
marked pea-comb.   This latter might have been 7 lbs. weight, and like the other,
was black-red in color.   The legs are dark olive green, with five claws on each
foot; shewing evidently a Malay origin, crossed probably with the Dorking.

cross-bred races to one or the other of the original parents.
This much, we say, is known to all poultry breeders. But
Mr. Darwin, whose facts are most reliable, whatever we may
think of his inferences, has also pointed out (we think for the
first time) that, besides this, the *very act of crossing* gives an
impulse to reversion, as shown by the re-appearance of *long-
lost* characters." That is, not only do the offspring of crossed
varieties continually tend to return to one or other of the
immediate parents, but the immediate progeny very often
exhibit characteristics *not found in either* of these parents, but
which can be traced back either to the primitive wild type
itself, or at least to some form far more ancient than the
actual progenitors, As this matter is both important to our
inquiry and highly curious, we quote the evidence on which
Mr. Darwin establishes the fact almost entire.

" My attention was first called to this subject, and I was led to make numerous
experiments, by M. M. Boitard and Corbie having stated that when they crossed-
certain breeds, pigeons coloured like the wild *C. livia*, or the common dovecot—
namely, slaty-blue, with double black wing bars, sometimes chequered with black,
white loins, the tail barred with black, with the outer feathers edged with white—
were almost invariably produced. I selected pigeons, belonging to true and
ancient breeds, which had not a trace of blue or any of the above specified marks;
but when crossed, and their mongrels re-crossed, young birds were continually
produced, more or less plainly coloured slaty-blue, with some or all of the proper
characteristic marks. I may recall one case, namely, that of a pigeon hardly dis-
tinguishable from the wild Shetland species, the grandchild of a red-spot, white
fantail, and two black barbs, from any of which, when purely bred, the production
of a pigeon coloured like the wild *C. livia* would have been almost a prodigy.

" I was thus led to make the experiments recorded in the seventh chapter,* on
fowls. I selected long established, pure breeds, in which there was not a trace of

---

* This and other references to Mr. Darwin's " Variation of Animals and Plants,"
are preserved for the sake of those who may desire to refer to that work.

red, yet in several of the mongrels feathers of this colour appeared ; and one magnificent bird, the offspring of a black Spanish cock and white silk hen, was coloured almost exactly like the wild *Gallus bankiva*.   All who know anything of the breeding of poultry will admit that tens of thousands of pure Spanish and of pure white Silk fowls have been reared without the appearance of a red feather.   The fact, given on the authority of Mr. Tegetmeier, of the frequent appearance in mongrel fowls of pencilled or transversely barred feathers, like those common to many gallinaceous birds, is likewise apparently a case of reversion to a character formerly possessed by some ancient progenitor of the family.   .   .   I have been informed by Mr. B. P. Brent, that he crossed a white Aylesbury drake and a black so-called Labrador duck, both of which are true breeds, and he obtained a young drake closely like the mallard.

"We have seen in the fourth chapter that the so-called Himalayan rabbit, with its snow-white body, black ears, nose, tail, and feet, breeds perfectly true.   This race is known to have been formed by the union of two varieties of silver-grey rabbits.   Now, when a Himalayan doe was crossed by a sandy-coloured buck, a silver-grey rabbit was produced, and this is evidently a case of reversion to one of the parent varieties.

"In the third chapter it was shown that at an ancient period some breeds of cattle in the wilder parts of Britain were white with dark ears, and that the cattle now kept half wild in certain parks, and those which have run quite wild in two distant parts of the world, are likewise thus coloured.   Now an experienced breeder, Mr. J. Beasley, of Northamptonshire, crossed some carefully selected West Highland cows with purely bred short-horn bulls.   The bulls were red, red and white, or dark roan ; and the Highland cows were all of a red colour, inclining to a light or yellow shade.   But a considerable number of the offspring—and Mr. Beasley calls attention to this as a remarkable fact—were white, or white with red ears.   Bearing in mind that none of the parents were white, and that they were purely bred animals, it is highly probable that here the offspring reverted, in consequence of the cross, to the colour either of the aboriginal parent species or of some ancient and half-wild parent breed.

"In the chapter on the horse, reasons were assigned for believing that the primitive stock was striped and dun-coloured : and details were given showing that in all parts of the world stripes of a dark colour frequently appear along the spine, across the legs, and on the shoulders, where they are occasionally double or treble, and even sometimes on the face and body of horses of all breeds and of all colours; but the stripes appear most frequently on the various kinds of duns.   They may sometimes plainly be seen on foals, and subsequently disappear.   The dun-colour and the stripes are strongly transmitted when a horse thus characterized is crossed with any other; but I was not able to prove that stripes are generally produced from the crossing of two distinct breeds, neither of which are duns, though this does sometimes occur.

"The legs of the ass are often striped, and this may be considered as a reversion to the wild parent form, the *Asinus taniopus* of Abyssinia, which is thus striped. As with the horse, I have not acquired any distinct evidence that the crossing of differently coloured varieties of the ass brings out the stripes. But now let us turn to the result of crossing the horse and the ass. Although mules are not nearly so numerous in England as asses, I have seen a much greater number with striped legs, and with the stripes far more conspicuous than in either parent form. Such mules are generally light-coloured, and might be called fallow-duns. The shoulder-stripe in one instance was deeply forked at the extremity, and in another instance was double, though united in the middle. Mr. Martin gives a figure of a Spanish mule with strong zebra-like marks on its legs, and remarks that mules are particularly liable to be striped on their legs. In South America, according to Roulin, such stripes are more frequent and conspicuous in the mule than in the ass. In the United States, Mr. Gosse, speaking of these animals says, 'That in a great number, perhaps in nine out of every ten, the legs are banded with transverse dark stripes.'

"The quagga is banded over the whole front part of its body like a zebra, but has no stripes on its legs, or mere traces of them. But in the famous hybrid bred by Lord Morton from a chestnut, nearly pure bred Arabian mare by a male quagga, the stripes 'were more strongly defined and darker than those on the legs of the quagga.' The mare was subsequently put to a black Arabian horse, and bore two colts, both of which were plainly striped on the *legs*, and one of them likewise had stripes on the neck and body.

"The *Asinus Indicus* is characterized by a spinal stripe, without shoulder or leg stripes; but traces of these latter stripes may occasionally be seen even in the adult; and Colonel S. Poole, who has had ample opportunities for observation, informs me that in the foal, when first born, the head and legs are often striped, but the shoulder stripe is not so distinct as in the domestic ass: all these stripes excepting that along the spine, soon disappear. Now a hybrid, raised at Knowsley from a female of this species by a male domestic ass, had all four legs transversely and conspicuously striped, had *three* short stripes on each shoulder, and had even some zebra-like stripes on its face ! Dr. Gray informs me that he had seen a second hybrid of the same parentage similarly striped.

"From these facts we see that the crossing of the various equine species tends in a marked manner to cause stripes to appear on the various parts of the body, especially on the legs."

Now applying these observations and principles to our own subject, we have seen that the pea-comb has been found on the Malay, on the Cochin, on the Malay and Cochin cross, on the Cochin and Spanish cross, on two mongrels, and—though less defined—on the game birds of India; and in *every case* excepting the mongrel, whose parentage was simply unknown, (with the almost certainty of a Malay cross in one case) and therefore cannot be considered exceptions, one or other of the *Asiatic* breeds is implicated. In fact, *each of the great Asiatic races*, when crossed, has been known thus to produce the pea-comb by reversion; while a third Asiatic race, which has had the conservative advantage of an insular locality, possesses it still. The conclusion is almost irresistible, that this pea-comb was a leading characteristic of some *ancient race of fowls*, the progenitor of all the gigantic Asiatic breeds. We say a *leading* characteristic; because while in the Malay, an admittedly ancient race, the feathered leg (if such be regarded as one of the original features) has long been lost, and also any tendency to transmit it, the inclination to revert to the pea-comb still lingers; and in the Shanghæ, which is feathered, and is also an ancient race, even the natural instinctive spirit of the male bird has almost disappeared, while still a tendency to this mysterious comb remains dormant in the breed. Very strong and marked must any character have been, to possess such wondrous vitality and permanence.

And now the question at once occurs, *What was that ancient race?* Was it some breed now long extinct—progenitor alike of Brahma, Cochin, and Malay? or was it, rather, neither more nor less than *the Brahma itself?*

D

We believe it was the latter.

This hypothesis may seem startling, and was not that formerly held by ourselves ; but we were gradually led to it by the evidence we have now laid before the reader, which has been collected during a period of many years, and on the ground of which alone it is now suggested. The real question is, What hypothesis best explains the proven facts? and it will be found that by this theory *alone* can every fact be harmonized with the rest and exactly accounted for. The identity of the crania so justly insisted on by Mr. Tegetmeier, is totally irreconcileable with the marked difference in other points, and the strong vitality of the pea comb as shown by reversion in crossing, on the supposition that the Brahma is a recent descendant of the Cochin ; but is quite so if we consider the Cochin to have diverged many years ago from the Brahma. It is well known that breeding Dark and Light Brahmas together often produces a buff tinge, and partridge could be bred in a few years with the greatest ease. So also, a cross back, either to the *Gallus Bankiva*, or the game bird of India, would produce a breed with long, smooth shanks, hard plumage, and drooping tail, closely resembling the Malay. In this matter each point of agreement, and each of difference, is easily and naturally accounted for.*

The objection that the breed was not imported earlier, is

---

* Much stress cannot be laid upon it, but it is still worth noticing, that the Malay has never been found to correspond altogether with the old *Gallus giganteus* of Temminck, so that some good authorities have doubted whether so large a bird ever existed as described by that naturalist. We have often thought it, however, far more likely that he was writing concerning some variety of the Brahma.

puerile. Malays were imported long before Cochins, while Cochins had scarcely any priority at all over Brahmas; and as well might it be contended therefore that Shanghæs were only Malays. We find, moreover, many testimonies to the fowl *having been seen* at different times, such as that of a clergyman who writes in May, 1856, "a relation of mine was looking at my fowls last summer, and on my telling him that Brahmas were considered by many only a variety of Cochins, he remarked, 'I remember Brahma-Pootras when I first went to India, more than *forty years since*, long before Cochins were heard of here: but they were considered a great rarity.'"* We could multiply statements to the same effect; and they are also said to have been seen in Ceylon, again implying that the racè is so ancient as to have reached various localities. At the present time it is well known there is a splendid large breed of fowls in Japan, but they are not yet "imported," and it may be years before they are.

All the facts, therefore, from which scientific deduction can be drawn, seem to point to one conclusion, against which not one argument can be urged. Then, going back

---

* An aged Indian officer who had read our first editions with interest, wrote us to say we were mistaken in our view, that the fowl " was the Chittagong breed, of which he had seen hundreds in India, only not so truly-bred as these new-fangled specimens." He did not see that the question was not one of *name* at all, and that his admission had established the one fact in dispute or which needed to be established, viz., that there *was in India* a pure breed of fowls resembling the Brahma. The strong probability is, that these Chittagong fowls had been imported into America long before, and from want of poultry knowledge become so degraded as to be unrecognizable. If so, this would account for the fact of Burnham's birds obtained by *crossing* from these degraded Chittagongs, being in some cases very near the true type, while yet uncertain in points owing to the mixture of blood.

to the history of the breed, and subjecting all the evidence alike to independent investigation, we find every account breaks down with ludicrous completeness, save that—confirmed in every point—which traces all to one mysterious pair! Yet there is no change—save in shades of color from the breeder's art—least of all is there degeneracy ; the Brahma came upon the scene, and it still remains, the largest fowl ever known. Was ever such a thing recorded of an ignoble race? But this fowl stood the test—a test which would have extinguished half our breeds.

And lastly, there are many who look to evidences of what they call "blood," and who will ask, Does *the fowl itself* bear out this theory? Does it—as we see it now—bear the impress of such a pedigree as we now suppose?

It does. It bears the stamp of nobility, plainly written. There are exceptions, caused by the past and present mistakes of breeders, and even judges, who would seek to alter it to the Cochin standard—wretched mistakes these are. But what we regard as the true and highest type of a Brahma cock, is in everything a lordly bird. Largest of all—dwarfing even the Cochin, though his closer plumage and splendidly perfect proportions make him appear smaller than he really is—he has, when in his prime, neither the heavy look of that breed, the stolid "country-man" air of the Dorking, or the conceited carriage of the Spanish fowl. He belongs to a nobler race ; and, colossal though he be, he treads the turf with the grand stride and regal bearing of the Game fowl. None but Game resembles him—no other bird can fight with him—no other bird dare stand before him !* And if we ask the reason it is not far to seek : the Game bird too is of royal blood—his pedigree can be traced back for ages.

Surely, then, it is no mere fancier's enthusiasm to affirm that our Brahma too derives *his* strength and courage from his unstained descent. Though never bred for fighting; though he has not, therefore, like the Game cock, in veritable black and white his quarterings to show, surely the evidence could not be more complete. He, too, can boast a lineage as high : the blood in his veins represents the original of a gigantic race : he is " the descendant of a line of kings !''

We may add that Burnham published a letter in September, 1870, apparently (though not confessedly) on account of the statement of facts and arguments we had issued in the first edition of this work, in which he affirms the black-breasted cocks, now admired by fanciers, to be a *third* variety or cross. " I am firmly of opinion," he says, " that this recently-marked, dark-breasted Brahma strain of fowls, which is so greatly admired among some fanciers, and of which several trios have of late come out from England, are skilfully bred in Ireland and England from the dark China hens they have had there, with the dark-plumed Grey Dorking cock, producing *this* variety (so closely resembling the latter in many points), and upon some of the first of which there not unfrequently

---

* We remember once selling a very young cockerel, which, the first night of his arrival at his new quarters, killed a large rat that had long troubled the fowl-house.

appeared the notable fifth toe of the Dorking, now bred off
again by cautious selections. . . . . I shall not change
my opinion in this matter until I can learn or unlearn more
than I *now* know of the ' Dark Brahma' strains of the present
time." To every breeder of the fowl, it will be at once
evident that the amount of knowledge here hinted at is not
great ; in fact, nothing could better show Burnham's ignorance
of *the fowl itself* than this opinion. The reference to
" Ireland" would appear to be pointed at Mr. R. Boyle, who
certainly was the first breeder who made the black breast
fashionable ; but none of his birds ever showed the Dorking
toe, or any other evidence of the black breast being so derived.
We further on speak of the Dorking cross as now and then
met with, and we had done so years before any other writer*
detected it—indeed, we have a strong suspicion that from us
Burnham " borrowed" the very idea†—but it was attempted
for far other objects than that stated by him, and every
breeder soon gave it up in disgust ; moreover, it was always
the Brahma cock and Dorking hen which were thus employed.
That Mr. Teebay for many years rejected from preference
numerous black-breasted cocks in favour of speckled ones is
known to all intelligent fanciers, and also the fact that every
good strain breeds *both*. We still prefer a slight mottling

---

* We say any other " writer," because Mr. Teebay had pointed out the cross to
us verbally long before.

† In "Burnham's New Poultry Book (pp. 165, 166)," he actually quotes from
this work, but cleverly avoids acknowledging it, by doing so through a *previous*
quotation from us by the "Canadian Poultry Chronicle," to which alone he
refers !

ourselves for breeding pullets, while no doubt the black-breasted cocks look best for exhibition. Either can be bred with the greatest ease ; and the assertions which Burnham elsewhere makes still more broadly, that most of the English birds exported to America bear evident traces of the Dorking, is an offensive and libellous falsehood, without any foundation whatever except the desire to puff off his own strain, which he does constantly. On the other hand, the persistence with which he attacks what he calls the "cross," and insists on the preservation of the *pure* Brahma, is, to say the least, amusing in the very man who has been the sole source of the supposition that this identical "*pure* Brahma" is *itself a mongrel* of his own creation !

CHAPTER II.

The Economic Qualities and Management of the Brahma as a Stock Fowl.

IN our introductory sentences we briefly expressed an opinion which we may here repeat, that the Brahma will ultimately be considered to occupy, in relation to other varieties of poultry, a similar position to that of the Short-horn breed amongst the various races of cattle ; or in other words, whilst by no means faultless, or combining in itself every possible merit in perfection, that it possesses a *greater* amount of real usefulness and value than any other pure breed, and is also capable in an eminent degree of communicating its good qualities to other fowls by crossing. We have recommended it in many cases to persons whose previous poultry-keeping experiments had not been satisfactory ; and in nearly every instance the fowl has fully justified the confidence reposed in it, and *earned* the warm encomiums of the parties concerned. At the same time the bird is *not* suitable for every case, and requires to be understood and rightly managed in order to yield a profitable result.

The progress of this breed in England is a remarkable testimony to its solid value regarded as live stock. Imported, as we have seen, in 1852, it shared in the "mania" (or "hen-fever" as Burnham calls it) which prevailed then and afterwards, and occasionally realized fabulous prices, sharing also with Cochins the comparative neglect which followed. But while

the Cochin, so extravagantly lauded at first as destined to
revolutionize English poultry, is scarcely ever heard of now
except as a fancy bird, with the Brahma the case is precisely
opposite. It has taken time for the fowl to become known, and
it was not till five or six years ago that its diffusion could be
considered at all general ; but a certain point once reached in
this respect, its growth in favor among *the people* has been the
most extraordinary poultry phenomenon of late years. Without anything approaching "mania," the entries each year have
steadily increased, until at nearly all shows the Brahmas now
form the most numerous classes exhibited.

A fowl which could thus grow in general popularity must
have many recommendations ; and in proceeding to describe
the economic qualities of the one in question, we may briefly
characterise it as remarkable alike for a handsome appearance,
great size, good quality of flesh, extraordinary fecundity,
remarkable power of adapting itself to the most varying
circumstances, and finally, an iron constitution.

The first point mentioned is not perhaps very material to
the present chapter, besides being greatly a matter of opinion;
and having already described the carriage of the male bird
as resembling that of the Game-fowl, we will here only add,
that the head of a well-bred Brahma pullet is more beautiful
in shape and expression than that of any other breed whatever, leaving the rest to the remarkably faithful portraits
which accompany these pages.

As regards size, however, we quote veritable facts when we
affirm that the Brahma surpasses all other breeds, not excepting
the gigantic Cochin. It is, indeed, apt to look smaller than

the latter, on account of the plumage in good strains being
much closer than that of the Shanghæ ; but stature and the
scales tell a different tale.   We have bred several cocks which
in their second year (the Brahma continues to grow during the
second season) reached thirteen to fourteen pounds, and we
have been told by Mr. Teebay of a cock he once had, which
when dead reached the enormous weight of nearly *eighteen
pounds !* We have seen several hens which weighed over 12 lbs.,
but the heaviest we ever had in our possession was 11½ lbs. ;
we have had several 10 lbs.

A full-grown cock of either breed cannot be regarded as up
to exhibition standard if he weighs less than twelve pounds,
while hens should weigh eight to ten pounds.   Cockerels six
months old should weigh from seven to nine pounds, and
pullets six to eight pounds. These last are very good weights,
and after long experience we have not the slightest hesitation
in saying that for all *practical* purposes birds which reach
these weights are to be preferred to heavier; but they will very
often be exceeded, cocks having been known to us (as just
observed above) which have reached in one case just over
eighteen pounds, while many hens have been known to turn
the scale on twelve pounds. Of course, if such birds are fine
in their other points they are very valuable for exhibition, and
there cannot be a doubt that the Brahma may easily be made
to attain a greater weight than any other breed, not excepting
the Cochin ; but as a rule we have found that moderate-sized
birds are healthier, more prolific in eggs, keep their plumage
in better order, and generally breed *finer and larger stock* than
the very largest birds.   We say as a rule, because there are

occasionally found birds which have grown very large without
any special feeding, and breed naturally a large stock, with no
apparent loss of fertility. Such are to be valued, and by their
means a large strain may be established and perpetuated; but
forcing size in this breed is to be especially condemned. The
effect is nearly always to make the plumage so*ft* and slack-
looking; and as the Brahma, unlike the Cochin, is a *close-
feathered* breed, one of its great beauties is thus to a great
extent lost.

The quality of the meat is also good. We have often heard
it stated that the Brahma "is not worth eating;" and there are
birds which, by carelessness, or a cross with the Cochin, have
degenerated into coarseness of flesh; but whenever even
tolerably well bred, the fowl will be found almost, and very
often quite, equal to the Dorking. There is certainly a little,
and only a little, less meat on the breast, but this is compensated by the extra quantity and *quality* of that on the
thighs; indeed many people think the leg of a Brahma cockerel
one of the best parts of the bird, and this great improvement
in what is the coarsest part of other breeds, counts very much
in estimating its value as a table bird. Altogether, the fowl
on the table is infinitely superior to nine-tenths of what can be
purchased at any poulterer's, and the skin should be either
white or of a delicate pink color.

We have a letter from Mr. F. Crook to the same effect.
"The flesh of a good Brahma," he says, "when cooked, is as
white as that of any Dorking; and with all the vaunted
superiority of the French breeds, I will engage to produce with
my birds, heavier fowls, flesh of equally good quality, and with

the finer parts equally well developed, with any stock they can produce." We must in fairness admit that we think Mr. Crook a little too laudatory here, the La Flèche having, to our fancy, a juiciness only equalled by the Game-fowl; but this breed is totally unsuited to our climate, and inferior in every other point; and that the Brahma can be bred equal to any other of the French races we are persuaded. Judges have perhaps been somewhat in fault respecting this point also; for in many cases the bird, owing to the decisions of arbitrators who do not understand the breed, has been bred unconsciously towards a Cochin standard, and the quality of the meat and proportions of the finer parts been thereby alike deteriorated. We are writing of the Brahma as it is *when unspoilt;* and while bound to admit that it cannot equal the Game fowl, and perhaps the La Flèche, in the sapidity of its flesh, our own experience is, that no other fowl surpasses it even in these points, while it has also upon the table a noble appearance which ought to go to the heart of materfamilias at once.

The fecundity of the hens is very great. It is true the production of eggs is considerably interfered with by the propensity to sit; but, in spite of this, there are many which will produce over 150 eggs per annum, which is a very high average. The tendency to incubate differs greatly in individuals. We have had hens which wished to sit when they had laid about twenty eggs, while others will lay from fifty to a hundred; and we have known cases where a hen has laid through the whole year with hardly a stoppage. There is no doubt whatever that egg-production has been actually *lessened* in Dark Brahmas by the keen competition of fanciers in breeding for "feather." Attention has been so exclusively directed to this point that others have been neglected and have suffered; besides which, exhibitors have actually sought to *postpone* the laying of their pullets as far as possible, in order to keep them in show condition. This, repeated for generations, has no doubt had a serious effect on egg-production; but what the breed is *capable* of is well shown by the following communication from Mr. John Evans, of Keynsham, near Bristol, for the truth of which we can personally vouch :—

"My experience of Dark Brahmas commenced in the spring of 1870; and being desirous to ascertain the productiveness of this class of fowl, I kept an accurate account for twelve months, day by day, of the number of eggs laid by three pullets—not themselves exhibition birds, though descended from prize ancestors of Miss Watts's strain. During the period named, the total egg-production of these three birds amounted in the aggregate to 629: and although I regret that I did not keep a separate account for each one, I am morally certain, from attentive observations that were made, that two of these birds produced each a much larger number of eggs than the third, and I am sure I am substantially correct in assigning to the two so referred to a proportion of 500 eggs out of the total number laid; thus showing a contribution to the egg-basket of 250 eggs each during the twelve months, as well as hatching and rearing a brood of chickens each within the same time. Two pullets from one of these birds, hatched on the 7th of March, commenced to lay within a day of each other, on the 16th and 17th of the August following, at the ages of five months and nine days and five months and ten days respectively, and continued to lay without intermission until the 11th of the following November, when I sold them. In the spring of 1872 I obtained from a gentleman to whom I had sold a pullet, a grand-daughter of one of the hens first named, and she commenced to lay early, producing an egg per day for five days; ceased the succeeding three days, and then, with a faculty for egg-production at least equal to that possessed by her maternal ancestry, laid sixty eggs in sixty-two days. I then disposed of her to a gentleman who, on my meeting him some few weeks afterwards, told me that her laying continued to be of the same character. One more example will suffice. From a sitting of eggs purchased from yourself in the spring of 1871 I have one hen, beautifully pencilled, which may be fairly termed an exhibition bird, and which has laid most abundantly. I much regret not having had the opportunity of keeping an accurate memorandum of her individual egg-supply, but I am satisfied it is equal to either of the instances named. No matter what the condition of the weather, wet or dry, cold or hot, there has been scarcely any intermission to her daily produce, not even during the moulting season just passed; indeed I have endeavoured, but without success, to prevent her laying so much. The feeding of my birds has been always of the most simple character, and I have never had recourse to stimulating food of any kind, such as is occasionally employed to induce laying.

Another great advantage in this breed is, that if broods are not wanted, the tendency to incubation, unlike the Cochin, is very easily checked. If the bird be taken from the nest *at once*, and put in a box-coop, or under a basket-coop on hard ground,

with plenty of water but little food, two days will often effect
the purpose, especially if two birds can be thus cooped together,
as their quarrelling will assist in the task.   If allowed to sit on
the nest a few days before being noticed, a week's confinement
may be necessary, and in less than a fortnight the bird will
usually lay again.   It is always best to check the propensity
for at least the first time it occurs, and that *instantly*, unless
the pullet has laid on into the new year; for if the bird was
hatched early, and desires to incubate, as she probably will, in
the autumn, she will often, if allowed to remain on the nest,
suffer a *second moult* the same year, which will not only be a
very severe drain on the constitution, but may hinder any
further supply of eggs till late in the spring.   Mistakes of
this kind will greatly affect the produce of the fowl.   Moreover,
Brahma pullets are not to be recommended in general for very
early broods, as they usually lay again in about a fortnight
after hatching, and consequently totally abandon their chickens
at about a month old, when they are far too young to shift for
themselves.   In May broods, however, this is no drawback, and
they commonly sit very steadily.   The adult hens as a rule
are exemplary mothers in every way, and will generally go
with their nestlings about six weeks, after which with ordinary
care even early chickens will do very well if brought into the
house at night.   Where many are reared, the pullets may be
employed even to hatch early broods, as no breed is so good-
natured and easily imposed upon by foster-children.   If
therefore a second bird that has just hatched only a few
chickens be cooped near the one about to forsake hers, a
transfer is in most cases easily effected, and the chicks thus

protected some weeks longer. As Brahma pullets lay with
great regularity at six to seven months old, and usually sit
within two months after, they may thus be made exceedingly
useful where a supply of early birds for market is desired.

The constitution of the chicks, when bred from *mature birds*,
is excellent. This point, as all fanciers know, has great
influence on the matter in every breed ; and we think Brahmas
have suffered perceptibly of late, in common with other
varieties, from the common practice of breeding from the last
year's chickens. In breeding for exhibition this is to a great
extent unavoidable ; but where Brahmas are kept as farm or
market stock, it will be found far the best to breed chiefly from
fowls which on one side at least are in their second year. The
chickens will then be nearly fledged and out of all danger at
about seven weeks old; but if bred from cockerels and pullets
mated together, as is frequently done, they will be very
long over the process, and often require much care. The little
cockerels in this case suffer more than the pullets, being often
nearly bare before the true feathers appear, and consequently
much stunted in growth, so as to be considerably smaller
than the pullets in the same brood. Chickens thus bred, in
fact, ought not to be hatched before April, when their parents
will not only be a year old, but their tedious fledging causes
little danger. The progeny of adult birds cannot possibly be
surpassed in hardihood, and may be reared with hardly a death
in the yard, if care be only taken to guard against cramp or
rheumatism in the legs during early seasons; and at three
months old the cockerels will weigh from 3½ lbs. to 4½lbs.
occasionally even more.

It will be seen then, that the Brahma has many and great merits, and takes high rank as a stock fowl, either for the supply of eggs or table use. But it will not answer in every case. In those special localities, for instance, where the taste of the public is so depraved as to insist upon *fatted* birds, the Dorking will be found far more remunerative, having a natural aptitude to accumulate fat which the Brahma (happily, to our liking) does not possess. If *meat* of good quality be desired, our fowl will well bear comparison; and it is a great advantage to be able to kill early chickens of a good size, without any extraordinary feeding or care ; but as a grease-producer it cannot compete with several other kinds. For this reason, independent of the senseless prejudice against *all* feather-legged birds, the breed would probably be found not well adapted to the London market.

Again, where eggs *alone* are wanted, the Brahma does not answer ; for if resolutely kept from having even one brood in the season, the poor bird often pines away and loses constitution through the excessive drain on its productive powers and the continual denial of its strongest instincts. Disappointment has frequently ensued from this cause, and the breed should never be kept under such circumstances, but Leghorns or some of the French breeds be selected. It is only where some fair proportion of chickens are wanted that the fowl shows to advantage ; then, be the soil dry or damp, the aspect cold or warm, the space unlimited or confined, it will thrive apace, and with ordinary attention produce a greater pecuniary return than any other we are acquainted with.

Should circumstances hinder the incubation of any particular

E

hen, she should be allowed to sit for about six weeks on nest
eggs, taking her off once daily as usual for the first half of
the period, and during the latter twice, in order to prevent her
being too much reduced. By this process, skilfully conducted,
the rearing of chickens may in some cases be dispensed with ;
but it requires some practical knowledge of fowls, and very
careful attention to the health, condition, and disposition of
each hen, to make it take the place of the natural process,
which should be always allowed when possible.

Another reason in favour of allowing each bird one brood,
is that all the feather-legged breeds are somewhat prone after
two years to accumulate fat internally. The Brahma is far
less liable to this than the Cochin ; but still, in confinement'
unless our directions for feeding be attended to, it is apt to
occur. In this case, as is truly observed by Mr. Crook, (who
has paid great attention to the subject) " the first parts to
suffer are the egg organs. The birds gradually become what
is called by poultry-men *down behind*, and if the tendency is
not checked the weight becomes so great that the hen walks
about with her hinder parts nearly on the ground, Penguin-
fashion, until at last actual rupture of the egg organs takes
place." Death may follow or not, according to the violence
and extent of the lesion ; but even if it survives the bird is of
course valueless for breeding. " Whenever such a prejudicial
tendency to fatten is noticed "—we again quote Mr. Crook
—" the best possible course is to let the hen keep to her
nest for at least a month whenever she becomes broody,
only feeding her once a day, and taking care that after hatching she does not get much food with her chickens. By this

rest of the productive system, combined with abstinence, the parts will often be brought back to their natural condition, and a cure effected." Prevention is however the best remedy, and if the birds are fed as presently recommended, such a condition can scarcely occur, as is proved by the fact that in our own experience we have never had a single case.

Candour also compels us to acknowledge, that Brahma cocks crow very often and *very loud;* and this will be a fatal objection in some cases where the fowl might otherwise be kept with profit. As Burnham has said of their eating, "they are amazingly fond of *crowing*, especially a *good deal of it;*" and this quality does not make the breed the most eligible for a town. We can only say that the crow is at least, in most cases, genuine and clear, not a hoarse gutteral growl like the Cochin's; leaving the reader to give the objection just what force he may.

The chickens, like all other fast growing fowls, have considerable appetites, though they *won't* eat "old hats" so far as we have observed. But the adult Brahma does not require a great amount of food, not nearly so much as the Cochin or Crêve Cœur, and scarcely so much as the Dorking. We have always found our own birds, when barley was five shillings per bushel, and other cereals in proportion, cost us about 1½d. per week each, having to purchase every smallest morsel they consumed, and of the best quality, as all poultry food should be. If there be foraging ground they can be kept for less. Even in the confinement of a town, therefore, the Brahma will yield a good return provided a brood can be allowed to each hen. When thus kept, however, they should be so fed, at only

two meals per day, as to be *always* eager for food, even at the
end of a repast. We have had visitors remark that our birds
"must be half starving," as they saw the hens fly up a yard in
the air when their breakfast was taken out to them; but we
have found by experience that this system of keeping them is
the best, not only for profit, but for real healthy condition.
In bad or cold weather, a little more should be allowed; but
we *never* allow our own fowls (except by oversight) to eat to
repletion. In a confined space such would always destroy the
profit of keeping poultry : it causes laziness, where it is more
than ever desirable that the greatest possible amount of
exercise should be taken, and in the case of Asiatics often
causes such distension of the crop as is never afterwards
really recovered from, leaving the organ in a relaxed state,
which is both unsightly and far from conducive to health. We
do not mean of course that the fowl should be really *starved*,
but simply that the supply should always be stopped whilst
"on the sharp side of its appetite." On this system the
Brahma can be kept in places where no other variety would
live six months, and will yield an unfailing supply of fresh
eggs when most wanted.

The farmer should seek to breed his own birds, as he will
probably find no exhibition strain, for reasons already stated,
which combine the merits of the fowl to nearly so great an
extent as may be the case with a little care in breeding to a
table standard. Many Brahmas will occur, for instance, with
the narrow Cochin breast; and some may be found which,
owing to a cross, have acquired the objectionable yellow skin,
and coarse flesh which usually goes therewith. But by selecting

the best layers from successive generations ; also choosing stock with good deep breasts, short legs, white skins, and small and pretty heads, and by rejecting for a few seasons the most faulty birds in these points, the real merits of the race will appear. It cannot be too often repeated, that to be a first-class table fowl, a fowl *must be bred for the table.* The Dorking has long been so bred, has been judged by size and kindred points, hence the size and proportions have greatly improved. The French breeds have been matured in a similar way. And we have satisfied ourselves fully, in the course of a careful study of the Brahma, that while owing to these circumstances, there are varieties which, as they stand, somewhat surpass it for table qualities, our fowl really posseses higher qualifications in this respect, in *proportion to the degree in which they have been cultivated,* than any other race known ; and that the most moderate attention from the market breeder would raise it to the very highest place in these special particulars.

In thus keeping the fowl for market purposes or for home use, a profitable result cannot fail if the preceding hints be duly attended to, and which may be summed up in a few lines. The breeding stock for the early spring should consist, on one side at least, of birds in their second year ; cockerels mated with pullets not being bred from till after April, and only fine, large-boned, vigorous birds being even then allowed to furnish eggs for the nest. Care should also be taken that such young birds are then selected as had *fledged rapidly* when chickens, as this point is apt to prove hereditary, and slow fledging is a great drawback to rearing. A pullet's *first* eggs should never be set, and unless she has been laying far into the spring, the

pullet herself should be *instantly* checked the first time she
desires to incubate ; but however often the tendency be
frustrated, each bird should be allowed one brood before June.
Finally, at least one half the stock should consist of hens
in their second year, from the fact already stated that they
lay better at that age than either before or after.   The eggs
of hens are also of much larger size.

When kept for eggs, the. stock should be selected in the
same way from birds which lay the largest, as they differ
greatly in this respect.   The average size of the eggs is about
the same as the Dorking; but some are no larger than those of
Cochins, while on the other hand many birds lay eggs equal in
size to those of the Spanish fowl.   Over-feeding, which has
already been condemned on other grounds, lessens the size of
the eggs materially.   Eggs from only the best layers should
be set, which in a generation or two, will easily produce a
stock, many of which will lay as much as 200 eggs per annum.
The farmer has this in his own hands, as these qualities are
always found more or less hereditary, equally with the arbitrary
points sought by the fancier.

The chickens will do well on good plain food, such as oatmeal for the first week or two, and afterwards sharps mixed
with barley meal.   They will yield a good return for milk if it
can be afforded.   The cockerels pay best if killed from three to
four months old ; but are splendid fowls up to ten or eleven
months, often appearing as large as an average turkey on
the table : indeed we prefer them dressed and served up in the
same way.   The pullets are delicious, being full of delicate
white meat on the breast, of better flavor and more juicy

than that on the Dorking fowl. The strains with the *smallest
and handsomest heads* are almost always the best in fineness of
flesh—at least so we have always found—a coarse cruel-
looking head being generally a sign of the opposite quality.
This is singular, as it is often the last sign of a remote Dorking
cross ; but it corroborates the generally received idea, that
while many first crosses are good, subsequent generations as
a rule retain more of the defects than the benefits introduced
by the experiment.

The first cross of the Brahma with a Dorking cock certainly
produces truly magnificent fowls; the largest, perhaps, that have
ever been reared. Chickens thus bred have been shown at six
month's old which weighed over 18lbs. the couple. By crossing
this mixed race again with the Houdan cock, chickens are
obtained which, though less in ultimate weight than the half-
bred Dorking, attain a still earlier maturity, and may be killed
at ten week's old of very good size. Both of these crosses are
well worth the attention of the farmer or market-breeder; but
their merits should be kept up by continually using the blood
of good and pure stocks, or the result, unless great judgment
is exercised, will be disappointment and deterioration.

Lastly, while all Brahma crosses make good layers, the
cross between a Brahma hen and a Spanish or Minorca cock
produces a fowl, generally black on the body, with dark striped
hackle, which for average fecundity surpasses any and every
fowl we know.

There are two affections to which Brahmas are rather more
subject than other breeds. The first is a tendency of the two
outer toes to be webbed together, which we believe to have

been derived from the strain of a leading exhibitor some years back, having never noticed it before, or in any yard since which had not employed a cross from the one in question. Most cases of this deformity admit of cure if the membrane between the toes be divided at about three weeks old, an operation which causes only momentary pain; but if left, one or other toe is generally hopelessly deformed. The other is a tumour at the point of the breast-bone, which, in our opinion, is generally caused by the Brahma's prominent breast being brought in contact with the hard perch. It is not very common, but almost every breeder who roosts his chickens will have one or two cases annually. It commences as a small sac filled with watery fluid; but sometimes the tumour is of a cheesy consistence, or one form may pass into the other. Any cheesy matter should be extracted; but all that is needed for the watery form is the simple treatment advised by Mr. Joseph Hinton, of drawing two coarse woollen threads, as setons, through the sac, and retaining them for a fortnight, moving a little daily. The bird should be prevented perching meanwhile.

We have occasionally seen deformed bills in Brahmas. Mr. Hinton states that he has noticed them as a consequence of in-breeding in Brahmas, Polish, and Malays. In the case of Brahmas, however, we have known it occur where two quite distinct strains have been crossed; and it is hence another very strong proof of the whole race being descended, as Mr. Cornish affirms, from one pair of birds.

CHAPTER III.

The Characteristics of Dark and Light Brahmas as bred for Exhibition.

AT various times considerable difference of opinion has prevailed as to the correct standard to which the Brahma fowl should be bred, not only in color and leg-feathering, but even in shape; and on some points we have ourselves seen reason to change opinions we formerly held. In attempting to define, therefore, the proper characteristics of perfect and pure-bred birds, we shall endeavour to indicate, directly or indirectly, where there is room for diversity of judgment; to give due weight to opinions that do not precisely coincide with our own; and, so far as our ability extends, to afford such information as may assist those who differ from us, while giving what we think solid reasons for our own views.

With regard to such disputed points, there is one general remark to make. Every breeder should by all means make himself acquainted with the proper characteristics of his favorite fowl, and have in his mind a definite idea as to the standard of perfection after which he aims. If such ideas have been formed intelligently, and on good grounds, they should not be lightly given up for the fashion of the hour, which can often not be depended upon longer than that of a lady's bonnet. It will often be better, and in the end even *pay* better, to sacrifice some prizes for a year or two, than to "give in" to the present fancies of second-rate judges, and *degrade* a stock in order to meet them. He is no true fancier—he is altogether unworthy the name—who merely seeks to win prizes : still less is he one whose only object is "to *have* the very best stock in England, and beat every one else,"—a truly miserable spirit and a miserable ambition this. For far higher ends do the real brethren of the craft breed and show their fowls. They believe that the feathered objects of their interest are calculated to render important service to their country ; that poultry is an important link in God's grand economy of nature, and destined to play no small part in that great "*food question*" which is ever pressing more deeply on the minds of those who study the social welfare of man ; and they patiently work and study, each in his degree, so to improve and maintain their favorite breeds as may make them better adapted to serve mankind, while at the same time their exceeding beauty shall be so increased as to render them still more attractive in the eyes of that softer sex to whose care and supervision they are so particularly adapted. One who works with such objects—and many do—will always be unselfish. When a brother fancier shows at last a better pen than his own, he will rejoice that a step has been gained ; and whatever knowledge he may have acquired will be cheerfully and readily communicated. A real fancier is a true patriot ; and if Jonas Webb is remembered and extolled for having improved the wool and increased the carcase of the sheep to which he devoted such attention, men like John Douglas, who raised the standard weight of the Dorking fowl several pounds over what was known before, or Mr. Hewitt, who has devoted years of his life gratuitously to aiding, by his vast experience and knowledge in awarding prizes, the general improvement of poultry, have also deserved well of their country, and done good work for their day and generation.

To breed to a really faulty standard, therefore, against the better judgment, is to give up all this for the sake of gain; and in the end no advantage will accrue, as the error usually cures itself within a short time, and then those who have pandered to it will have some trouble in recovering their lost ground. There was a remarkable example of this in the case of our Brahma fowl. A few years since, dread of the vulture hock was carried to such an absurd extent, that almost *bare legs* became the fashion, and well-feathered shanks could scarcely win, except before one or two of the best judges. Nearly all were carried away by the stream; so much so that we ourselves, beginning to breed at that time, could not get well pencilled birds even moderately feathered at any price. But it did not last. After a season or two the tide turned; those who had given way to it had to *get back* the lost feather as best they could; and we are sorry to say that many of them did not scruple to breed *hocked* birds, and show them with the hocks plucked, in order to wrest the prizes from those who had bred fairly, and were not willing to use such means of gaining exhibition honors.

But on the other hand, it should not be forgotten that such fixed ideas as we have been advocating may be *carried too*

far. We have said they should not be lightly given up for
the fashion of the hour: but there is such a thing possible
as riding a hopeless tilt against the collective judgment
of all else beside. This can never succeed, and is to be
avoided : as in most things, so in this, the middle path is
the safe one. If for years the opinion of breeders, and of
the best judges, sets evidently in one direction, it is seldom
wise to attempt to resist it, as has been the case with several
individuals we could mention. Except there be very strong
reason for it, such a course will at length degenerate into
mere ignorant obstinacy, and can only result in continuous
defeat. We value our own opinion, and we would have every
one else to value his ; but the opinions of others, when time
has been given to test them, must in all cases be treated with
respect ; and in most instances, when they do really appear
to be mistaken, they can be, if not too recklessly opposed, so
modified as not to be injurious.

In shape, style, and carriage, the Dark and Light varieties
of the Brahma should be precisely similar. Some few years
since the Light variety had degenerated greatly in these
particulars, owing in our opinion to the comparatively few
who bred it in comparison with the Dark ; but of late
magnificent specimens have been shown, and Light Brahmas
now bid fair again to rival the Dark, not only in size and
shape, but in general popularity. The following remarks with
regard to shape will therefore apply to both breeds.

The head of the cock cannot be too small in proportion to
the body. Scarcely a point is of so great value as a sign of
high breeding ; and as we have before remarked, we have

also found that as a general rule a small head is accompanied by fineness of flesh, which in a breed like the one in question is a point never to be lost sight of. The top of the head should be rather wide, causing a slight fulness over the eye, which in the pullets causes that peculiarly arch expression for which they are remarkable, and which the cock should partake of to as great a degree as possible. The eyebrows must on no account, however, be so prominent as to cause a cruel or Malay expression. The whole head should be rather short, a long head looking bad, and disfiguring many of the present American birds.

The pea-comb is peculiar, but is simply described as resembling three small combs joined into one, the centre one being higher than the two outside. It is very difficult— in the cock especially—to get this point into perfection until a strain has been bred for years. No pure strain indeed ought to breed a solitary comb in which the peculiar triple character is not perfectly distinct ; but there is a constant tendency to grow too large, or crooked, or otherwise mis- shapen, which requires to be guarded against like any other fault, if even tolerable symmetry be desired.

In a perfect comb the centre ridge should be absolutely straight, and the whole so low as to be perfectly firm and free from shaking, however quickly the bird moves his head. We would prefer half-an-inch in height, but even three- quarters, if straight and well-shaped, makes a beautiful comb : above that we should say there was a tendency to getting too large. With regard to the shape of the comb opinions differ. Some prefer a uniform rise from the front towards the back, ending in a peak something like that of the Hamburgh, though not so sharp or defined ; and this is the original and present American type. But we like far better to see the comb, after rising for half or two-thirds of its length, decrease again towards the back, thus forming a kind of arch ; and this form of comb not only, as we think, looks better to the eye, but is far more likely according to our experience to breed well than the other, which has a tendency to grow larger each successive generation. This form of comb has now become the generally accepted type for a Brahma.

In our first chapter we have explained that the original Brahmas bred both single and pea combs. Dr. Gwynne and some others perpetuated the single comb, but the pea-comb soon became the favorite, and was *easiest bred*, proving it to be the most natural to the breed. Since then the single comb has all but disappeared, and never in any class now receives prizes at shows.

The comb should be handsomely set above neat and cleanly cut nostrils, the beak being rather short, thick at the base, and with a very decided curve : but too much curvature, or what is termed a hawk-bill, is a great blemish, giving a sinister aspect to the bird.

In all the original Brahmas the deaf ears fell below the wattles—and this point was even mentioned by Dr. Bennett as a characteristic of the breed. It is often seen so still, and its perpetuation should be carefully sought as far as possible ; but a prominent place cannot of course be given to so secondary a character.

Just below the head, the neck hackle should start well out

with a full sweep, making the point of junction between the
head and neck very distinct by an apparent hollow or
depression. The hackle can hardly be too full in our opinion,
and should descend low enough to flow well over the back
and shoulders. Perfection in this particular adds very greatly
to the noble carriage and appearance of the bird, while a
scanty or too short hackle is a decided fault, though it may be
occasionally condoned for the sake of other points.

The neck may be either rather long or rather short,
according to the general style of the bird all over; each has
its beauties and its admirers, and each has contended success-
fully in the show-pen. The short neck harmonises best with a
square compact body, somewhat resembling the Cochin in
character; while a somewhat long neck, well arched, and
combined with the proper type of tail, as is well shown in
our plate, gives, in our opinion, a more commanding and noble
appearance. Such birds used to be bred by Mr. Teebay, and
their lofty stature and bearing, with their proud and springy
gait, were something to be remembered. We sometimes see
them even now, and all that needs be said in regard to this
point is, that the whole contour of the bird should be such as
harmonises well and makes a pleasing whole.

The back should be wide, and flat across, with scarcely any
apparent length, the saddle appearing to rise almost from the
base of the hackle. A round back is a great deformity, and
a very narrow bird is not to be tolerated in a pen. The
saddle cannot be too broad, and ought to *rise* well towards
the tail; without this there cannot be true symmetry and
proportion. There has been much improvement in this

point of late ; but a few years back we have seen cocks with
the back and saddle sloping down towards the tail, which
looks particularly bad, being contrary to the haughty carriage
so conspicuous in this breed. The longer the saddle feathers
are the better.

The tail of the Brahma cock originally was very peculiar
but it is now become exceedingly rare to see it approaching
perfection. Most breeders at one time appeared to aim at the
horizontal soft tail of the Cochin, with which the short neck
(as already observed) has become associated, and the appearance of the fowl thus greatly altered from what it originally
was. Such tails are therefore admissible enough for exhibition,
and the fancier must breed and show the best he can get
according to his own ideas. The great difficulty of getting
back the old type may be imagined from the fact that we
have in our possession a letter from a well-known Birmingham
winner, stating that he thought such tails exceedingly ugly,
and "never bred from such a bird !"

This proper and characteristic tail has been variously
described, but most usually it is stated that "the sickles
should open out into a fan." Sometimes it is said that the
whole tail should thus open, and the usual standard of
comparison has been the tail of the black-cock. By the
kindness of Mr. Teebay, however, we are able to give a clear
description of the caudal appendage as it used to be, and
which we must regard as the perfect *standard* or type, however we may fail to approach it now. "The true inside tail,"
he says, "I like closed, except the two highest feathers
(sometimes *four* used to be so.) These should be very broad,

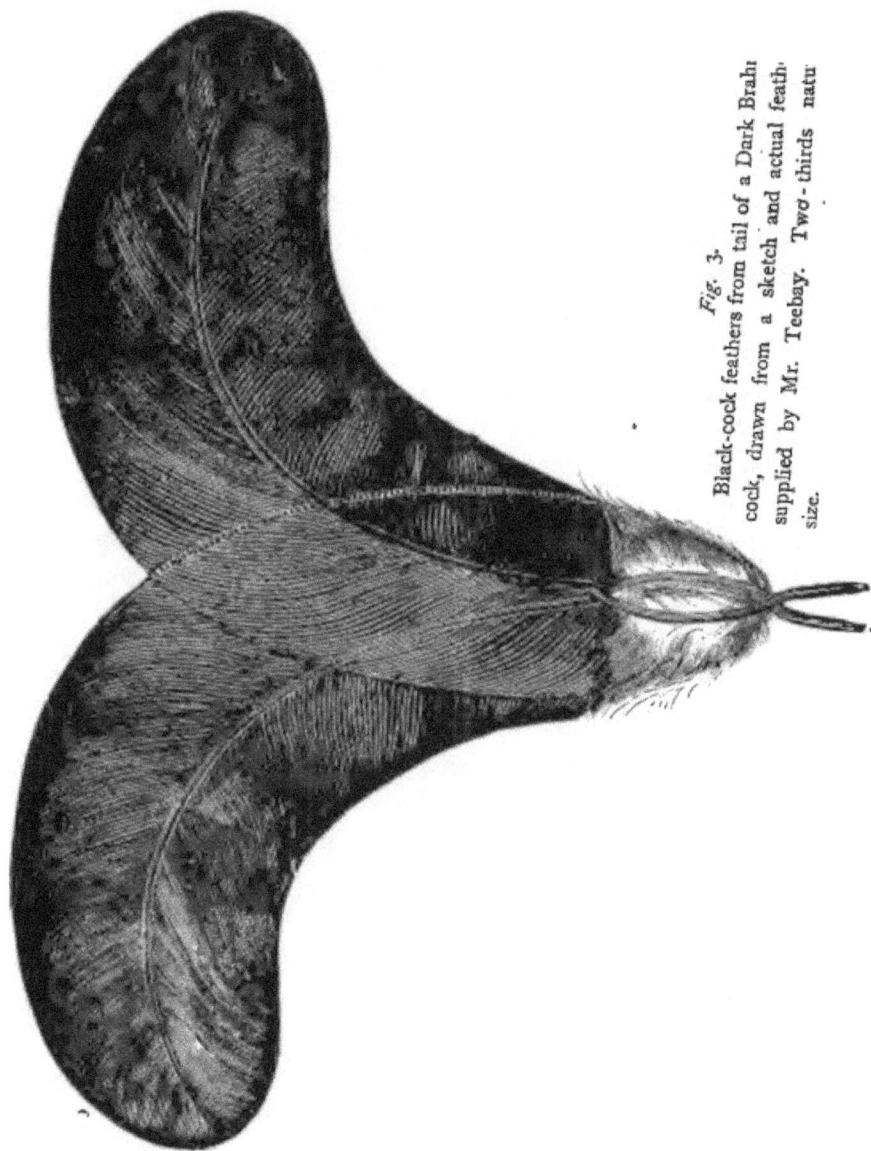

Fig. 3.

Black-cock feathers from tail of a Dark Brahma cock, drawn from a sketch and actual feather supplied by Mr. Teebay. Two-thirds natural size.

and lay nearly or quite *flat*, not too long, and the ends turning outwards each way, and projecting on each side *through* the curved or sickle feathers. Such feathers are never seen except in tails set much more upright than most exhibited now. They were very subject to be broken in the exhibition baskets or pens, on account of their projecting through the other feathers. The whole inside tail spreading out, as was also often seen, I do not like. I have frequently noticed the feathers crossing in the lower part and *re-crossing* again higher up, as in the sketch. When there are two pairs the higher pair is generally rather smaller, and they do not actually cross, though there is always a similar peculiar bend, which is I believe caused by their being set into the rump so near to each other, and growing together whilst the young quill is hardening."*

We add a drawing of these black-cock feathers, from a sketch and actual specimens kindly sent us by the same eminent judge and breeder, and which once belonged to some of his old birds. If the drawing be raised till nearly upright, what is meant will be readily seen; and the resemblance to the tail of the black-cock will appear far more striking than if the whole tail be opened out like a fan. Indeed, the heads of the pullets, the character of their pencilling, and the tail of the cock, with the feathered shanks of both sexes, present a cumulative amount of resemblance to the grouse, which

---

* Since this description was first published, we have had fanciers very politely question if such tails could be bred. It may be sufficient to say that the bird represented in the plate answered to the description exactly, with a *perfect* comb and every other characteristic of a true Brahma.

furnishes one of the most singular examples of what Mr. Darwin calls "analogous variation" in widely different species, known to us throughout the whole range of natural history.

The breast ought to be deep, full, and broad, if rather projecting so much the better. The breast-bone or keel should be deep and well down between the thighs. The shoulders of the wings should not be too sharp and prominent, but sufficiently so to make the back, when the bird stoops, a little hollow from shoulder to shoulder, and give a handsome proportion. The wings should be of medium size, and well tucked up under the saddle feathers, their points pressing tightly into the fluff on the thighs. If the cock is thus perfect in his " side-rigging," the effect—in spite of his size—will be particularly neat and trim. A slipped or disordered wing is a very great blemish, and tells greatly against a bird, however perfect in other respects.

The thighs should be furnished with an ample supply of the plumage so well. described as " fluff," but somewhat harder and more compact than in the Cochin. The lower feathers should in our opinion cover the hock joint, but curling well round it. Some breeders seem still to prefer the bare hock, or anything rather than get an occasional falcon hock : but general opinion is now returned to the former dictum, that the hocks of feathered fowls should be well covered with soft, curling feathers. Falcon hocks are to our fancy a great eyesore ; but only stiff feathers, projecting so as to form a prominent spur upon the limb, are to be so regarded ; and we would rather that even this should be permitted, than the disgraceful practice of fraudulent plucking, which we regret to observe has lately been practised by even eminent breeders, should become more general.

The shanks ought to be short and as well feathered as possible, so the bird be bred honestly without showing vulture hock. Both the outer and middle toes should be feathered; but sometimes very heavily feathered birds have the middle toe bare, and are not therefore to be discarded.

Too short shanks in the cock look decidedly bad, but it is rather hard to fail in this respect. The shank-feather should "stand out" well, not take a perpendicular direction, else it does not show properly. We need scarcely say that the thicker the shanks are the better. Very large cocks are generally somewhat long in the leg, and if the length be not *too* great we do not object to it, provided it is not, as is frequently the case, associated with too long a back or other defects in shape.

The shape and carriage of the hen should correspond with that of the cock, allowing for the difference of sex. Her head should in particular be as small as possible, this point being of much greater moment in her case, with the same slight fulness over the eye, giving to the face an expression we can only describe as "arch," but at the same time peculiarly sweet and gentle. We like the head short and well arched; in fact, as already said, almost exactly that of a grouse, with the beak also rather short and curved, but not too much so. The neck in her case short, and with the hackle spreading out very full at the base, and flowing well over the back and shoulders. The back flat, wide and short, as in the cock, with a very broad and ample cushion resembling somewhat

that of the Cochin.   There is however this difference, which
is characteristic, that whereas the cushion of the Cochin
rather droops at the extreme end, burying the tail, the
cushion of the Brahma rises to the last ; the short tail rising
nearly upright out of the end, so that the lower feathers of
the tail are further behind than the upper.   Many of the
pullets lately shown have been nearly destitute of cushion,
and narrow in the stern almost like a Spanish hen : these
birds have often won from the excellence of their pencilling,
but we cannot consider them good Brahmas.   The shoulders
should not be too sharp, but very neat ; and the wings
tightly held to the body, and well tucked into and nearly
buried in the cushion above and the fluff of the thighs below.
A "slab-sided" bird is not to be tolerated.   Breast as broad,
deep, and full as possible, with the crop low down, and the
breast bone well down between the thighs.   The fluff ought
to be very abundant and stand well out, covering the hock
precisely as in the cock.   A Brahma hen *must* be short
on the leg : legginess may occasionally be tolerated in an
otherwise good cockerel ; but a leggy hen is of little value
either for show or for the breeding yard.   In both sexes the
shanks should stand as wide apart as possible, any approach
to knock-knees being instantly disqualified; and the feet
should be rather large, with straight well-spread toes.

We have now to describe the distinctive markings of the
separate varieties; and in regard to the Light, which we shall·
take first as that first seen in this country, we have to
acknowledge the kind assistance of both Mr. Pares and Mr.
Crook, well known for their success as breeders and exhibitors

of this beautiful fowl, and who have most cheerfully placed their knowledge and experience at our disposal.

The head of the Light cock should be white, the hackle silvery white, with a *distinct* black stripe down the centre of each feather. The shoulder-coverts, back, breast, thighs, and underparts white on the surface, but the fluff or underpart of the plumage dull grey down to the skin. The secondaries or outside wing feathers white on outer web, and black on inner web, causing the wing to appear pure white when folded : the primaries or flights black. The saddle feathers may be either white, or (and this is much to be preferred) white *lightly* striped with black. Tail coverts glossy green black, those next the saddle being silvered on the edges. Tail rich glossy green black : if the two top feathers be edged with silver it should be preferred as a characteristic point already referred to : but this cannot be insisted on. The shape of the tail is already described; in default of that conformation, what would be sickles in another breed should diverge laterally like the tail of the Black-cock ; but in either case it should be nearly upright, and the tail of the Cochin is not to be sought after. Shanks *bright* yellow, the feathering white slightly mottled black. Perfectly white shank feathering is if possible to be avoided.

Our illustration, by Mr. Pares' kindness, is drawn from a photograph of one of the most extraordinary birds ever shown, and in all but one point is a faithful likeness : "Sampson" was in our opinion certainly much too light in the hackle, and we have therefore darkened the stripes, which in him were barely perceptible, to what should be considered

a correct standard.   The saddle we have not altered, as a
white saddle has already been explained to be quite admissible.   In style and symmetry the bird was a model ; and his
noble carriage will not soon be forgotten by those who knew
him before the accident which terminated his existence.*

The hen should have a pure white head, the bright red of
comb, deaf ears, and wattles contrasting very distinctly :
hence good condition is specially important in showing this
breed.   The neck clear white, distinctly and *darkly* striped
down each feather, the black stripes ending *clear and round* at
base of neck, so as to form a kind of dark necklace.   Breast,
back, saddle, and in fact the whole body a clear white surface,
with an under ground-colour of grey.   In the hen the primary
or flight feathers alone are usually black.   Tail coverts white ;

---

* The career of this bird is worth remark. Bred in the spring of 1863, he
commenced his career in 1864, with a commendation at Brighton (all the prizes
going to dark birds in a mixed class on that occasion). He took first prize at
Manchester the same year, and in 1865 won the first prizes at Woodbridge, Win-
chester, and Birmingham ; besides second at Brentwood, and high commendations
at two other shows—in all three cases against dark Brahmas. In 1866 he won the
first prize at the Poultry Club's Show at Rochdale, and throughout the year took
first at Woodbridge, Salisbury, Reading, Cirencester, and Shoreham (against
eighteen entries), winding up by taking first for the *second* time at Birmingham,
when he won the most valuable silver cup given at that show. He was entered
the same month for Manchester, where he would doubtless have taken his old
place, as he had just beaten the actual winner at Birmingham ; but on the way
to the show a dog gnawed a hole in the basket and worried him to death, at the
age of 3½ years. It must be remembered that in his time breeders of Light
Brahmas were few, and separate classes for them at shows also far between,
so that the bird had not the same chances of winning he would have had now.
He was never once beaten by a bird of his own color ; and though in our opinion,
as we have said, too light in the hackle, was in all else an almost perfect model of
what a Brahma should be.

LIGHT BRAHMA HEN.

BRED AND EXHIBITED BY MR. F. CROOK.

the tail itself black, except the two top feathers, which should if possible show the characteristic white edges alluded to in Chapter I., but this point cannot be insisted on. Legs bright yellow; the feathering white, very slightly mottled with black.

Our illustration is a faithful representation of what, after some years, still remains the best hen we ever saw : she was also one of the largest, weighing very nearly 12lbs. It is within our own knowledge that Mr. Crook refused £20 for this bird ; and one of equal merit would realize that sum at almost any time. Her beautiful cushion and ample fluff were things to be remembered : yet there was not a trace of the Cochin formation so often seen in so-called Light Brahmas.

In both sexes of this variety, any decided tendency to yellow is a great defect. It exists naturally in some strains, and is different from the sun-burn which in long sultry seasons will sometimes occur even in good white birds. Pullets are also liable to occur with splashed or spotted plumage, instead of clear white ; such are very inferior, and if the black is of any considerable amount it should be a disqualification.

The head and neck of a Dark Brahma cock are very similar to the Light, the head being white and the hackle striped, but somewhat more so than in the Light breed. The back is nearly white; a little black appearing here and there, while between the shoulders the black ought to predominate, but is nearly hidden by the hackle flowing over it. The saddle feathers are like the hackle, silvery white, striped with black.

Many breeders prefer only a *little* stripe in the hackle and saddle feathers, and such are most showy birds for exhibition, while they will often breed good pullets if other points are correct : but on the whole we greatly prefer a good distinct dark stripe in every feather. As the feathers approach the tail the stripes get broader, till they merge into the tail coverts, which are rich glossy green-black with a margin or lacing of white. The effect of this is very beautiful, while a "mossy" appearance of the coverts is not only unpleasant to the eye, but is inferior for breeding pullets. The tail itself is pure black with a rich gloss, any white being a great blemish. This fault is hereditary in some otherwise good strains, and is we believe caused by a remote cross with the Dorking. Sometimes, instead of a green lustre to the black of the cock's wings and tail, the feathers show *purple* reflections.

The wing coverts are black, forming a distinct black bar across the middle of the wing, while the ends of the secondaries, or the feathers which appear when the wing is closed, have a large black spot on the end, making the top edge of the wing also appear black. The remainder of the secondaries are white on the lower half and black on the upper, but the black of course is not seen. The flights are all black except a narrow fringe of white on the lower edge. There is often a little brown or bronze towards the top of the "bar," and at the end of the secondaries. As hereafter explained, this is often very useful for breeding dark pullets, and if not too plentiful is not to be considered a defect, but if very conspicuous is almost a disqualification. There is also often a portion of brown on the shoulders and back :

in such positions the colour should be condemned, being both
unsightly and objectionable for breeding.

The breast may be either black, or black very slightly
and evenly mottled with white, though a black breast is now
almost necessary to win at any good show, and certainly looks
much the best. The thighs and fluff either black, or black
very lightly tipped or laced with white. The shank feathering either black, or mottled black and white, corresponding in
either case with the breast. The best and handsomest colour
for the legs is deep yellow, inclining to orange ; but this can
never be obtained except on a grass run, and if the legs are
moderately yellow it is sufficient ; many of the best Brahmas
being reared in small yards.

Our coloured illustration is drawn from the most perfect
specimen we have ever yet seen or bred. Being hatched very
late (May 27) it was impossible he should grow very large,
though he reached a very fair average size, but every point,
so far as we could discover, was absolutely perfect. He
possessed the grouse-tail as already stated, a beautifully small
and *perfect* comb, clear colour, intensely solid black stripes,
and the deepest colour for breeding, without the least brown
in any part whatever.

The colour of the hen somewhat varies, according to the
taste of each individual fancier. Mr. Boyle, for some years a
very successful exhibitor, describes it in "The Practical
Poultry Keeper" as a "dingy white ground, very much and
closely pencilled with dark steel-grey." The effect of this is
very beautiful, giving the appearance of a frosted or silver-
grey ; but there should be no appearance of pure white in the

plumage except in the margins of the neck-hackles.   Pullets
of this colour are in perfection at about six to eight months
old, but next season often acquire a very dingy tone which we
much dislike.   The hens also are of a dingy colour except for
a month or two after moulting ; but we have bred a few birds
of this colour which retained their clearness of tint to the last,
proving that with care in breeding the objectionable dingy
tone might be got rid of.   A more serious fault is that this
colour is very apt to breed pullets with necks almost white for
some distance down ; and even below that very thin and uncertain in stripe.   These light-necked birds generally breed
worse and worse ; but the evil can easily be checked by
choosing birds for breeding whose heads are distinctly marked.

A few years since some breeders, amongst whom was Mr.
Lacy, preferred a decided brown colour for the hens ; a tint
which breeds true with much less trouble than the clear.   This
tint is occasionally shown with success, but being in the
opinion of most fanciers much inferior in beauty to the clear
colour, has nearly if not quite gone out of fashion, and it has
lately become an accepted axiom that a clear ground-colour is
the proper one for a Brahma.

Another colour is that which used to be shown by Mr.
Teebay, and is generally much admired when seen in perfection, as it sometimes has been again of late years.   The
ground-colour in this case is itself a steel-grey, and the
pencillings or markings a rich black, so intense as to show
green reflections like the tails of the cocks.   Sometimes there
is a slight cast of chestnut in the ground, but the intense
colour of the pencilling prevents this from looking the least

dingy, even when the birds moult out as hens. The ground then often shows the chestnut tone, with a slight purple cast, but the birds look wonderfully rich even then.

Other shades of marking also occur ; and on the whole what we prefer is a variety of the first or silver-grey colour, in which the grey of the ground is of a perceptible *bluish* cast, and the pencilling itself so dark as to be nearly black. This colour, which may be denominated the blue-grey, usually moults out tolerably clear, the bright grey only giving place to a slightly duller slaty cast, which makes the hens of this colour show better than any, unless the very dark pencilling may be an exception.

Between these all shades of colour and marking may occur, and often patches of the different schools will be found in the same bird, arising from sudden crosses between different strains. This we especially dislike : we would never condemn a pullet because bred to another colour than what we prefer ; but we do like any colour or marking, whatever it is, to be pure and alike all over the body, and a bird distinguished by much broken colour or unevenness of marking ought never to win in a good class.

The very shape of the pencillings also varies, being in some strains almost straight across the feather, whilst in others they follow the outline and partake of the character of lacings, one within the other, as on the breast. In this point too we think a somewhat medium character the best looking, the pencillings being moderately curved, but not to too great a degree. On the breast they are fully curved or laced in all strains. But whatever shape, colour, or character the pencilling assumes, *precision* is of great importance, obscure or irregular markings being very inferior in effect.

A few American fanciers seem greatly to admire a feather for Dark Brahma pullets which, besides the regular pencilling, has a defined *edge* of dull white, considerably lighter than the

Breast.   Flat of Wing.
Fig. 4.

rest of the ground-colour. Two such feathers we have represented in Fig. 4, from specimens sent us some time since by Mr. E. C. Comey, of Quincy, Mass.* The effect is rather peculiar, and gives a sort of artificial appearance of gloss to the plumage, particularly on the cushion ; but it seems to us

---

* By the courtesy of the publishers, these and other drawings of feathers are reproduced from " The Illustrated Book of Poultry."

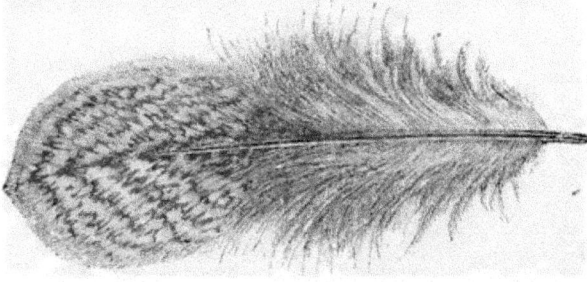

Hackle.

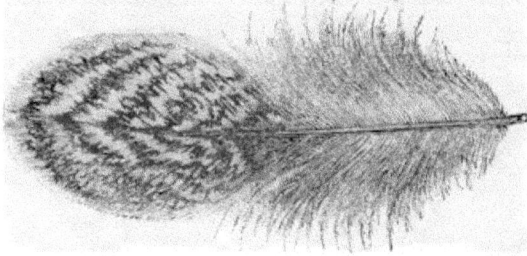

Breast

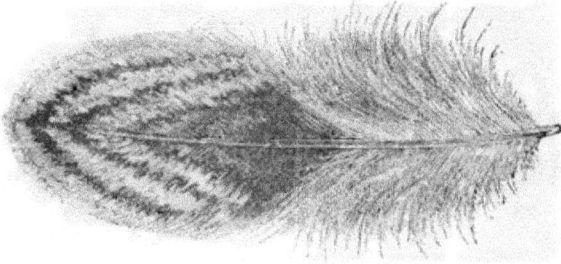

Flat of Wing.

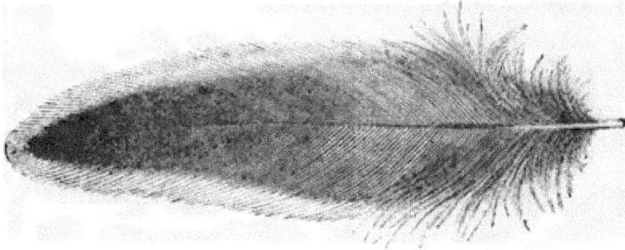

Cushion.

Fig. 5.—FEATHERS OF DARK BRAHMA HEN.

MR. L. WRIGHT'S DARK BRAHMA PULLET.

"PSYCHE."

to destroy the uniform look which most fanciers seek, and we should prefer to have the feather coloured alike all over. There is no difficulty in breeding this white edge, if desired, as traces of it are every now and then occurring in almost every yard, from which it can be easily perpetuated.

We also append drawings of feathers taken from one of the best hens we ever saw of the blue-grey colour already spoken of, plucked at the age of twenty months; but considerable variation from this type is quite admissible provided the plumage be uniform, and pure according to its own standard.

The head of the pullet or hen is silvery grey, or white striped with black. Lower down the neck the stripes get broader, till at the bottom they are very broad, nearly covering the feather, and ending in blunt or rounded points. The rest of the plumage should be pencilled, according to one or the other of the standards above described, the pencilling especially reaching up to the throat, and one of the chief points in a show bird being that the character and depth of marking on the breast approaches that of the rest of the body as nearly as possible. The tail feathers alone are black, except the top ones, which are pencilled on the edge. The shank feathering of the hen *ought* to be perfectly pencilled as on the body; but this is not by any means universal, and in a fine bird we would not insist upon it, though it is desirable. The shanks should be deep yellow, with or without a dusky shade.

Our coloured illustration is taken from the best pullet we have ever seen. She was not remarkably large, weighing only a litttle over 8 lbs. but was of beautiful shape, and singularly free from brown. Her colour was an exquisitely pure blue grey;

G

and the markings on the breast could hardly be distinguished
from those on her cushion.   Being hatched in March, by the
time she won at Birmingham she had lost much of that
beautiful bloom and purity of colour, which was remarked by
the artist as "extraordinary" at the time her portrait was
taken.

Such are the colours of Brahmas as now exhibited, and birds
which do not come under the distinct heads of Dark or Light
would have no chance in the show pen whatever.   But it will
not have been forgotten that the first pair of birds were *grey:*
and while we see and feel the great beauty of the two classes
into which they so soon merged, we have always regretted
that the old grey Brahma should have no recognised standing.
The colour was not uniform, being usually more or less of a
grey speckle over a white ground, but was almost always
beautiful, as any who have seen some of Miss Watts' grey
birds will admit; that lady being the only one, so far as we
know, that maintains the old grey stock.   Very often the
pullets come most exquisitely laced over the body, and the
purity of the grey is always remarkable, while it moults out
clear to the very last.   No birds breed true to colour with so
little trouble in mating ; and we think, for this season, that as
the fowl becomes popular on English farms, it may probably
be the original *light grey* Brahma which is preferred ; for without great care the Dark birds are always tending to this colour
more or less, proving their origin to have been thus derived.

CHAPTER IV.

*The Practical Breeding, Rearing, and Management of Brahmas
for Exhibition.*

THERE is an odd kind of fascination about breeding
Brahmas that we have not felt with regard to other
fowls. Not that the young birds are handsome—far from it:
it is the very reverse fact that adds the charm; the chicks,
especially the cockerels, being so unconscionably ugly at
a certain age that they seem made for scarecrows and
nothing else. As therefore their hidden beauties begin
late and slowly to develope themselves, being visible to the
experienced eye weeks or months ere the casual spectator
can discern anything but the "lean plucked chickens"
Burnham so graphically describes, there is a pleasing excitement about the business difficult to describe, but by no
means hard to understand. You stand in your yard, and
looking at your biggest cockerel, mentally pronounce him
the very ugliest wretch you ever saw in your life—but—
you don't know what he *may be!* Week by week you
watch his great body settle down lower on his long legs: his
wing feathers, once in such hopeless disorder, you get right
after awhile with infinite pains; and when at last that tail
which seemed as if it *never* would grow begins to develope,
and the bird slowly acquires his adult plumage and gets into
condition, your hopes rise high as you see that he is "quite

as good as last year's Birmingham cup bird, Sir," and hope
that the cup may be his in due time. It may or not be—
for oftentimes the whole class at an exhibition will show such
a marked improvement over the previous year that a far
better bird is required to win : but some such experience as
this belongs to every fancier, and adds a pleasant feeling of
excitement to a pursuit that is in itself, when rightly and
reasonably followed, not only interesting and beneficial to
the individual, but useful to the community of which he
forms a part.

The attainment of both these desirable ends, however, will
depend entirely upon the manner in which the business is
commenced and conducted. In very rare cases we have
known persons to have purchased at some show a winning
pen of birds, which have not only maintained subsequently
their high position, but have been the progenitors of first-
class stock. This can however only happen when the pen,
besides being good for exhibition, is also properly mated for
breeding ; and very rarely is this the case. If the first prize
cock and the first prize hens at an exhibition be purchased
separately, it is many chances to one against their breeding
good stock ; and since we have turned our attention specially
to this breed we have had dozens of letters from persons who
have spent large sums in this way, and afterwards given up
the fancy in disgust ; whereas, if they had been content
patiently to *study the fowl* for themselves, or enlisted the
judgment of some experienced breeder, they might not only
have saved many pounds useless expense, but derived from
their yards both profit and innocent gratification.

Before going into details it may be well to lay down a few
general principles: the very first of which is, that no written
instructions can supersede that *personal study* we have just
advocated.   Fowls, like men, have their "crinks and cranks,"
and often some strongly marked individuality will baffle all
calculations, and when discovered, needs to have special
allowance made for it if success is to be attained.

Again, it is most desirable if possible in commencing a new
strain, to provide at the outset several unrelated pens. By so
doing the breeder may keep his strain *in his own hands* for
many years, until it is thoroughly established and its qualities
defined, while year by year, if he knows what he is doing,
he will come nearer to his wishes ; but if he is obliged to buy
a cockerel every year for "fresh blood," he does *not* know
what he is doing, and may spoil the result of years of patient
labor, by some glaring fault lying latent in, and imported
quite unsuspected by, an unlucky cross. We know a strain of
Dark Brahmas, for instance, which breeds very good stock
when kept to itself ; but the cockerels when crossed with
other strains very often produce at first pullets disfigured
with large white splashes, and cockerels with almost white
breasts. Even the skilful breeder is constantly liable to be
deceived in this way ; and it is from sad experience, that
whenever we breed from a strange cockerel we "hope for the
best and expect the worst," as is recorded of the old woman
who was compelled unwillingly to go to a fresh grocer for
her pound of tea.

If fresh blood be really required to recruit an old and good
strain, no pains are too great to ascertain what the birds are

likely to breed. Whenever possible the new stock should be chosen from *the breeder's yard;* and if young birds, the purchaser should ask to have the parents (if alive even the grand-parents) pointed out to him. If not bred by the vendor, he should ask the parentage, and when practicable see the yards thus indicated. Should the birds be older, he should for similar reasons ask to see their progeny (if any), and ascertain *how they were mated* in order to produce them. In all or any cases, both the excellencies and defects that appear in either generation should be carefully noted, and the observer should endeavour to form a judgment as to what circumstances either have been owing. And finally, in thus crossing into an established yard, the most perfect birds possible should be procured, unless some particular defect be needed to counteract one of an opposite nature. This may appear a great deal of trouble; but to avoid spoiling a yard once brought to high excellence is worth it all, and it is just the careful observance of such particulars which makes the distinction between the skilled and careful breeder, and the man who thinks "money can do anything," and finds that *it can't,* at least in poultry breeding.

But in commencing an altogether new yard, it is not necessary, nor even always desirable, to purchase perfect and high-priced show birds. In the first place, as already explained, even such birds will often breed a comparatively small proportion of good chickens, unless got from and matched by one breeder, which is not preferable in all cases ; whilst on the other hand excellent results may often be attained with very moderate stock, provided they be so selected that the defects of the cock shall *counteract those of the hens.* Again, size in Brahma stock, if adult, is not of the importance that might be imagined ; for the breed, as we have already noted, has such a wondrous *vitality,* or power of recovery in this point, that magnificent chickens may be reared, with good feeding, from small parents—a fact which we think cannot be affirmed of any other fowl.

It will be found by experience, that with one exception, the cock has the most influence upon the fancy points, while the hen has the most upon the form and size.   Hence it is infinitely better to breed from small cocks and large hens than *vice versa*—indeed we always rather like small cocks for their liveliness and vigor.   Hence also the reason why legginess in the cock is of less importance than in the hen, though even in her it may be counteracted.   Hence also a narrow cock and very wide hen are more likely to breed well than the contrary.   And it is the cock especially to which the breeder must look for defects or perfection in the comb, for the yellow leg which is so great a beauty, and, with the one exception already hinted at, for all the *finer points* of the breed.

That exception is the *pencilling* of the Dark breed.   With regard to this feature, very long experience has convinced us that the influence of each sex is by no means equal, but that there is far more probability of breeding good chickens from a perfectly and darkly pencilled pullet or hen, and an untried or second-rate cock, than from a badly coloured or pencilled hen, and a cock of the most perfectly pencilled "blood" that can be procured.   There will probably be some

bad and some good in both cases, but the average will be
as stated.   If very bad in marking, therefore, a Dark hen
had better be discarded altogether : if even second-rate,
we should expect very few good pullets from her, but if
unusually fine in shape and carriage it may be worth while
to breed from her with a good male bird, for the sake of
the cockerels, and the stray good pullets which may come
by chance.

A bad-combed hen, also, may be bred from if a cock with
a very small fine comb can be procured, with the probability
of success.   But any actual deformity of the frame, such as
round or crooked backs, must be "stamped out" at once, or
the consequences may be lasting and grievous.   There is a
minor blemish of this kind which is very apt to prove hereditary, in the shape of small and crooked toes, instead of the
firm, straight, spreading feet which alone become such a
magnificent fowl.

With regard to more venial faults, in choosing a breeding
pen let them be mutually and most carefully compensated.
If the cock have a drooping back and saddle, let the hen be
very high towards the tail ; if his hackle be short or scanty,
let that of the hen be unusually sweeping and full.   Any
white stain in the ear lobes (which is a blemish, though not
a disqualification) is very apt to perpetuate itself; and if
therefore any of the breeding stock possess it, particular
care should be taken that the other sex has had no sign of it
for generations.   If the hen is at all long in the leg, the
shanks of the cock must be *particularly* short, or nearly all
the progeny will be long-legged to a certainty.

To breed heavy feather, the best plan at commencing is to mate a heavily feathered and hocked cock with hens nearly bare-legged. We have had hocked birds we valued highly for breeding purposes, though we cannot express our utter scorn and contempt of those who would pluck them for show; but in general such cockerels, good in colour and other points, may be obtained at a very moderate price. Some hocked birds have very little shank-feathering—such are only fit for the kitchen, any hocked bird used for breeding being also heavily feathered; when, if mated as described, there will be very few hocked chickens, the great majority being beautifully feathered, with soft, curling, but well covered hocks, just right for the show pen. The cross between a scantily feathered cock and hocked hens is not quite so good, according to our experience, producing more hocked pullets; whereas the other cross seldom breeds more than one-fourth to one-eighth of hocked birds. The progeny, however, must be mated with peculiar care; for if birds so bred be penned together, there will often be many hocks re-produced owing to reversion, though the birds themselves be unexceptionable in appearance. Chickens bred from a hocked parent, therefore, if fully feathered, should be mated with birds from some other family bred with no taint of hock, and very *slightly* less feathered than themselves; when the progeny will commonly be feathered about the same as the better furnished, hock-bred parent. By attending to these precautions, splendid feathering may be obtained, with very little trouble from vulture hock. It cannot be denied that the proper way of breeding would have been to maintain the proper heavy feather by selection, without aid from hocked birds at all : but the recent fashion of bare legs, and the subsequent use of hocks to remedy its effects, have so contaminated every yard, that it is better to make a *known* experiment which can be controlled, than to purchase and mate heavily feathered birds with an *unknown* amount of hocked taint, and which will be almost certain to produce many hocks, as we have found to our cost.* In a very few years, by attending to the precautions above described, all tendency to hock may be effectually eradicated, without any loss of feather.

In breeding for size, it is best to select a very short, compact, deep-bodied cockerel, which need not be large, and mate him with long-backed hens, even if their legs be rather longer than ordinary. Although length of back is a decided fault, such a cross will generally breed well; the hen appearing to supply the frame, which the cock fills out to the proper proportion. In this way we have bred pullets magnificent in shape, which weighed 9 lbs. in November, from hens only about 7½ lbs. weight, but whose length of frame supplied the necessary material to work upon. Long, rangy, large-boned cocks may also be mated with compact, short-legged hens for the same purpose ; but we should prefer the mating first mentioned, as generally producing better results.

---

* A few years ago, we had many letters complaining that nearly all the eggs sold by a very successful exhibitor produced chicks with hocks nearly sweeping the ground. A friend of ours grimly remarked that he had got "a new breed with wings on their legs." The result in other yards recruited or commenced from this stock may be imagined.

Some of the finest chickens in point of size which we ever had were reared from the eggs of a pullet; but subsequent and larger experience has convinced us that the general opinion is correct, and that the best chickens as a rule are produced by mating either a two-year old cock or a cockerel with hens in their second season. The great point is that such chickens *fledge* more quickly, and hence get to their growing stage at an earlier period. Cocks may however be mated with pullets without any hesitation, and such a pen has the advantage that it usually produces a good proportion of pullets in each brood, while hens mated with cockerels often turn out too many male birds; but every such rule has marked exceptions. To mate cockerels and pullets, as we have already said, is not advisable; but we would not shrink from it with fine strong-boned birds, hatched before the middle of April; and one of the largest cockerels we ever had, weighing 8 lbs. at five months old, was bred from such a young pen. When young birds are thus mated, however, care ought to be taken that all of them have grown up strong and without illness; that the cockerel did not suffer from leg-weakness in *his* young days; and especially that the practice be not repeated with the progeny of the same stock next season.

Many breeders have much too great a fear of "breeding in-and-in." We have already hinted at the consequences of always depending on "fresh blood;" and would ten times rather breed from near relations than from unrelated birds of bad quality. If three, or even two separate breeding pens can be provided, the fancier may go on for years without a purchase, and as long as he can breed birds good enough he had better do so. Parent and offspring, or even brother and sister, may be bred from without injury, provided the experiment be not repeated until several years have elapsed, and *fine birds* be chosen : but if any fault exist it will of course be greatly aggravated by such a *concentration*, as it were, of the faulty blood. On the other hand, beauties may be also concentrated and fixed in the same way, as was done in the celebrated " Favorite" family of Shorthorns. No breed has such stamina as the Brahma ; and we never knew evil result from breeding between relatives, unless it were foolishly repeated, which ought never to be done, or unless small and weakly birds were thus bred together.

If the breeder seeks to reproduce the peculiar " black-cock" feathers, the hen as well as the cock should be chosen with reference to this object. Some hens will be found in which the top feathers of the tail lie nearly flat over each other : such are the birds to be selected, with a cock showing any similar disposition to flatness in the top pair of quills.* The difficulty is, that such birds may not unlikely be inferior in other equally important characters, and hence have to be rejected ; and recovering a character so much lost as this is, in the case of at least Dark Brahmas, can only be the work of time, unless the fancier has the good fortune to find a bird with the feature in question, and other points also perfect, when a little care will fix the point speedily.

---

* The cockerel represented was bred in the third generation from the first selection of stock with a view to the grouse tail. The second year a hen was bred with an upright tail, the top feathers of which lay perfectly transverse, and from this hen, with the same male parent, was bred the cockerel in question.

The chief difficulty in breeding Light Brahmas is to obtain a sufficient amount of black marking in the hackle, without producing colour where not wanted. The natural tendency of most poultry is to breed lighter and lighter ; but if, to counteract this, cocks be chosen with densely-striped hackles, and saddles also striped, and mated with dark-necked hens, the almost inevitable result will be pullets with backs and other parts spotted or splashed, and cockerels with black spots on the fluff, in the wing, and other undesirable places. The best plan, at all events at commencement, will be as

Fig. 6.—Black Hen Hackle for Breeding Pullets.

follows :—To breed pullets, put a cock with narrow but tolerably distinct stripes in his hackle, saddle quite clear, and leg-feathering nearly white, with hens so darkly striped in the neck as to be unfit for exhibition, or if they can be got so dark, entirely black, even in the very fringe, as in the feather shown in Fig. 6, which was plucked from a fine American hen. From such a cross, pullets with hackles resembling the feather represented in Fig. 7, will be produced, and so far as regards colour nearly every pullet will be fit to show ; while a fair number of good cockerels may also be expected, though many will not be marked enough to be considered really perfect birds.

To breed cockerels for showing, on the contrary, a cock should be selected with stripes in his hackle of a very solid character, and defined stripes in the saddle also, if possible; and mated with hens either the proper colour or slightly too light and cloudy in the hackle, and entirely free from any colour on the back. From this mating hardly a cockerel will miss as regards colour, but many of the pullets will have backs more or less speckled; except in rare cases, when birds seem to "breed well" with no trouble at all.

Fig. 7.—Correct Hackle for Light Brahma Pullet.

The colour of the grey under-fluff should also be carefully examined. It will be found that this varies, in some birds being of a very dark grey, and in others of a very light pearly grey. In many cases the dark grey under-colour goes with the darker surface-marking, but this rule is not by any means universal; and if two birds be on the surface apparently *both* too dark to be mated with success, for fear of producing dark splashes or specks, yet supposing one—say the cock—be of a dark under-colour while the other is light, the experiment may often be made with success. We think, in fact, this rule will usually be found safe; but as we once knew a marked exception, we do not like to state it too broadly. By attending to this qualifying point, in a few years it will be possible to breed from the *same* stock both cockerels and pullets of a beautifully-marked character, the cocks usually having white saddles with barely perceptible traces of black; and by then always mating well-marked birds on *both* sides, but with under-colour rather dark and light respectively, this valuable quality may be perpetuated.

The Light Brahma is so extensively bred in the United States—more generally, perhaps, than any other breed—that a few remarks on the American and English types as compared become almost necessary. The American birds are, as a rule, much longer in the leg and back, and therefore less compact in shape, than the English; but (no doubt as a direct consequence of this) are bred to a far larger size. An imported cock was shown in 1872 which exceeded *eighteen* pounds' weight, and twelve and thirteen pounds are not at all unusual weights for hens. Hence American birds make valuable crosses to gain size; but we must confess our own predilection for the square and compact English form, when bred to a satisfactory size, which there is no real difficulty in doing. The American birds also differ somewhat in colour, being described by United States' fanciers themselves as almost exactly the colour of new milk when drawn from the cow, not the bluish colour of milk when skimmed of the cream. In England, on the contrary, this very pearly or bluish-white colour is most preferred, as it is also by some American breeders, being much less apt to run into deep straw-colour in the cocks. American birds are also very often rather long in the head, which somewhat detracts from their beauty of expression. Probably the most perfect standard of perfection would lie between the two extremes as regards shape; and there is little doubt that overmuch seeking for short-legged cocks has seriously diminished in size several good English strains : but neither, on the other hand, can we admire the gaunt, lanky, raw-boned look of some American importations we have seen. We should rather advise the mating of fine long-bodied American hens of ten or twelve pounds' weight, with a broad-backed, short-bodied, and very short-legged English cockerel of a good pearly colour, taking especial care the male bird had a broad and rising saddle. From such a cross, if rightly chosen for breeding colour, valuable results may be secured. A long, large American cock may also be put with compactly-built hens for the same purpose ; but we would prefer the cross first mentioned.

The only cross that is likely to be met with in choosing Light Brahma stock is that with the white Cochin, which we are satisfied has contaminated more or less very many birds. As this has been denied by some experienced breeders, we think it right to state that we have the avowal in writing of a well known winner at Birmingham, that some of his best birds "were bred from a Dark Brahma cock and white Cochin hens ;" and of course such a cross must not only affect his own strain, but would communicate the taint to any others which might be recruited from it. The evils of the experiment would be more apparent after two or three generations than at first, as chickens quite correct in marking are often produced by such a cross ; but the effect of reversion is

always seen afterwards in single combs, dark or sandy
patches of colour, light hackle, and deficient breast. The
latter is on the whole the best test of a cross, which may
be also detected in many cases by the ground colour of
the plumage being white instead of grey; and if the two
defects be found together we should regard the evidence of
a stain more or less remote as perfectly conclusive. Another
very characteristic evidence of a Cochin cross is the shape of
the cushion, which in Brahmas rises more and more till it
rises into the nearly upright tail, whilst in crossed birds it
frequently rather droops over; but as true Brahmas occasionally present this conformation, too much stress must not
be laid upon it.

Light Brahmas keep much cleaner than any other fowls
which have much white in the plumage; but still they cannot
of course be kept so as to show to advantage either in or very
near a town. They require a clean, fresh grass run to do
them thorough justice; and when thus happily situated are
the most strikingly handsome of any fowls we know. If in
good condition, they will then require no preparation whatever for exhibition, but should be shown just as taken up off
their runs, simply washing their feet if dirty. If these
advantages cannot be had, they may still be kept in beautiful
condition in well gravelled or sanded yards, or on bare earth,
provided there be an ample and *absolutely* dry shed, well
supplied with finely sifted road dust or gravel, mixed with
finely cut and very clean straw. The latter not only en-
courages them to scratch and cleanse themselves, but deepens
and brings out the yellow tinge of the legs, and helps to keep

H

the other materials dry.. This last is specially important : for
all fowls show a perverse disposition to revel in *damp* rather
than dry earth ; and the result on white plumage may be
imagined. If kept in the smoke of a town it is very difficult
to show Light Brahmas with credit ; and though much may
be done by good washing, it will be better that the fancier
should content himself with the equally beautiful Dark breed.

It is also necessary to provide plenty of shade for Light
birds, otherwise even good, pure white strains will become
sadly sunburnt in dry seasons. As we have remarked, there
is a yellow which exists in some strains, and which nothing
can bleach ; but what is simply sunburn may in some cases ·
be improved by covering the yellow parts with chloride of
lime, very fresh and strong, made with water into the
consistency of cream. This should be washed off in half an
hour or less, *thoroughly*, with solution of hyposulphite of soda,
the whole being rinsed out with blued water only. If care be
not taken, the remedy will be worse than the disease, owing to
the caustic power of the lime ; and washing fowls removes so
much of that beautiful gloss which gives half the charm to·
their plumage, that it is far better to provide such shade as
may render any treatment unnecessary.

In breeding Dark Brahmas also, the constant tendency to
breed lighter must be allowed for ; and therefore, to maintain
the character of any strain it is ever necessary to provide
depth of color on one side or the other: in fact either the cock
or the hens should if possible be a shade darker than the colour
desired. Mr. Teebay, who some years since carried all before
him, and exhibited birds equal or superior to any seen now,

always attributed his success to the fact that he "bred the darkest birds together," which soon gave a character to his strain no other possessed; and if depth of pencilling be desired the same plan must be followed still.

The selection of hens or pullets will be comparatively a simple matter. The fancier should consider what colour and character of pencilling he prefers out of all those to be observed at shows, and then procure birds as near to it as possible. If they be, as above remarked, a shade darker than the fancied colour, it will be all the better, provided the *character* of the pencilling be the same. It is necessary however to distinguish between pullets and hens; in the case of silver-grey birds especially, which as hens often look so brown and dingy, that it seems almost impossible to believe they were of that exquisite colour so admired by many in the young pullets. Such brown birds will often breed good stock; nevertheless, as the dingy colour is the great drawback and blemish of the silver-grey school, if hens can be obtained free from it so much the better. In any case, the birds should be well pencilled over the breast, or it will be long and tedious work getting dark-breasted pullets from such a stock.

There is almost always a little tendency in Dark Brahma pullets to show the shaft of the feather white about the shoulders and front of the breast, causing a slight appearance of streakiness, as in the silver-grey Dorking. This tendency will increase if not watched; and when allowed to develope causes an unsightly appearance, being most conspicuous, by contrast, in the darkest coloured birds. Hens or pullets very much disfigured in this way should therefore be discarded; or, if employed for the sake of unusually fine shape or colour, must be most carefully mated with cocks quite free from streak: otherwise the produce will be nearly all thus marked; and the tendency may get so much developed that it may be almost impossible to breed it out again, the whole body showing the white streak down the centre of every feather in a most unsightly way. A little about the breast used to exist in nearly all pullets, but careful breeding has nearly banished it, and there should be many pullets perfectly free from either streaky or light breasts in any good yard.

Hens or pullets with very large coarse heads, of a "sour" expression, should in nearly every case be refused for breeding stock. Such a strain is generally crossed some time back with the Dorking, and to get coarse heads is to lose one of the chief beauties of the Brahma breed. A hen with this defect has in most cases large, coarse pencilling also; and only when the size, shape, and carriage were unusually fine, and pencilling also good, would we experiment with her, choosing for the purpose a particularly fine-headed male bird.

It is the choice of the cock that is the chief difficulty in breeding Dark Brahmas; for those differences in colour and marking which in the hens are so apparent, are in him only partially perceptible even to the most experienced eye, and to most persons not at all. There is not a breeder who has never been disappointed in his expectations from some noble-looking bird; the different strains being so crossed and blended that unexpected tendencies are often developed, and baffle all calculation. Still, there are some general principles which make success at least likely to be the reward of him who will observe them.

In breeding silver-grey or blue-grey pullets, the cock ought, if possible, to be entirely free from brown, even in the wing-bar. Purple reflections in the tail are also improper, the right colour being a very bright greenish black, while the bar on the wing should appear positively green. The more black there is towards the front part of the back the better, and the hackle and saddle-feathers ought to be solidly and *very distinctly.* striped, as in the feathers shown at Fig. 8, which are

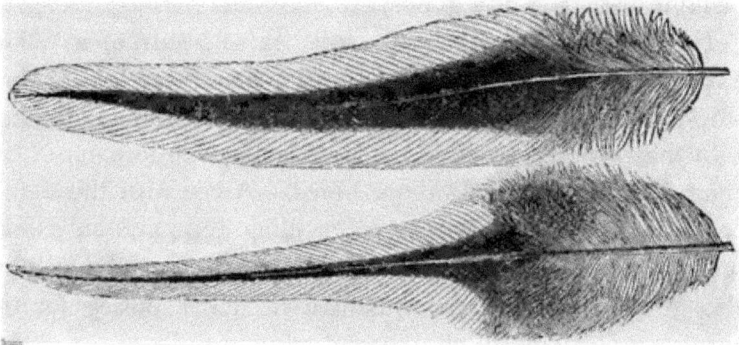

Fig. 8.—Hackle and Saddle Feather of Dark Brahma Cock for Pullet breeding.

plucked from a bird of our own that hardly ever bred a bad chicken. Supposing the bird perfect in these respects, almost all will depend on the colour of the under parts, as compared with the breast ; and Mr. F. Wragg,* formerly manager of Mr.

* He speaks thus : "I wish to repeat, that for breeding I select a cock with all the under parts perfectly black. I especially dislike to see the fluff on the cock's thighs with white in it. Many of the chickens from such a parent would be very bad in colour, showing light streaky feathers on the breast."—*Practical Poultry Keeper,* p. 111.

Boyle's yard, lays great stress on the breast, thighs, and fluff being pure black, which seems at first sight reasonable enough. We are, however, satisfied from experience that it is to this rule, or more particularly to the principal stress being laid on the blackness of the *fluff*, that the white heads and pale breasts so frequently seen in silver-grey pullets are due. If a black-breasted cock can be procured, the fluff may be black with no ill result ; but while black fluff is common, an *entirely* black breast is more rare : and if the bird have the *least* white mottling on that part, while the fluff is black, the effect will almost invariably be that the pullets bred from him are very dark behind, but too light on the breast and head. On the other hand, we have always found that a cock with the fluff slightly mottled produced better pencilled birds than the pure black, provided the *middle* of every feather were quite black, and all the white confined to the edges. Very often the *shaft* of the feather shows white in the fluff of the cock, and birds so marked will almost invariably breed just such "streaky" pullets as described. But if the shafts and whole centre of the feathering be a rich black, with only a lacing of white at the tip and edges, no such result need be apprehended ; and all that has to be stipulated for a probable good result is, that the breast, whether mottled or black, be darker, or at least fully as dark, as the thighs, especially under the throat ; the hackle well striped ; and that his hens have good pencilled breasts. This last is after all the most important point, for without *good breasts in the hens* the best cock in the world cannot be relied upon for pullet-breeding. A bird of first-class pullet-breeding blood may indeed breed various beautifully-marked birds, even from streaky-breasted hens but these will be exceptions, not the rule, and such is not good or scientific breeding. We have often heard it said that only a few well-marked pullets can be relied upon. This is not correct, except to the random breeder; and we can state unhesitatingly, from experience, that any one who will breed his own stock with judgment for a few years, can easily mate up pens that will scarcely produce 10 per cent. of pullets, which as regards marking leave anything to complain of.

It is a singular fact, that by continually selecting cocks with wings perfectly clear from brown, a tendency was for a long time always developed to *increase* the brown, thus producing the very thing so carefully shunned. The brown so developed in the cockerels was however very different from that in the darker strains, being of a dead or rusty tinge, and often stained or mingled with white. This fault also was, however, vanquished by patience and care, and for several seasons past we have succeeded in breeding cocks perfectly clear in the wing, yet of the most intense colour, and unexceptionable breeding qualities.

In breeding for the dense, very dark pencillings, as well as for the preceding colour, a cock should be selected with the stripes at base of the hackle a-particularly dense black, and the saddle also well striped. Particular attention should be given to the shafts of the feathers, both in hackle and saddle, and if they be very white the bird should be rejected. Indeed, this precaution is necessary in breeding for any colour; but most of all in this, because the dark colour of the pullets will make any streakiness more conspicuous. We do not think we ever saw a cock quite free from white streak somewhere in the shafts of the saddle or hackle, but there should be none for some distance from the tips, or we have generally found the bird bred streaky chickens. As the saddle merges into the tail-coverts, the black stripes ought to become very broad, and beautifully sharp at the edges, with glossy reflections ; such a bird will rarely disappoint. The fluff is best of the same brilliant black in centre of the feathers, with a slight lacing of white ; and the breast may be either black or very slightly mottled. The best breast for breeding pullets of this colour, according to our experience, is marked with round white spots the size of pepper-corns, evenly distributed over glossy black ; but a black breast, with the fluff described above, will also breed good pullets, and for producing cockerels is much to be preferred. Particular attention should also be given to the front part of the back, where it is covered by the hackle. If there be plenty of black, *dark* pullets may be confidently anticipated, the other points mentioned above being correct ; but they will often be *too* dark, merging into almost solid black on the back, with dark blotches about the breast ; though this is not always the case by any means. But if the hens also are dark, a cock should, if possible, be selected in which these black feathers of the back are *laced with white* on the edges ; and he will in most cases, fluff and saddle being right, breed beautifully-pencilled birds. The wing may or may not have a very small amount of colour in it, but not so much brown, as a metallic, glossy, copper *bronze.* This should be situated towards the top of the wing-bar, and at the ends of the secondaries or quills of the wing, but not in so great a degree as to be very readily seen. The reflections of the tail and wing should be either green of a *bluish* cast, or of a purplish shade ; we have found both breed beautiful pullets, but there is always some difference between the tails of the dark cocks and of the preceding strains.

The breast of the cock *should in all cases be as dark, or rather darker, than the fluff.* For breeding cockerels, perfectly black-breasted birds should, if possible, be chosen, that colour being much more valued in a show-pen ; but for breeding pullets alone, we still say that a *very slightly mottled or laced breast is best*, provided only it be darker than the fluff, that the black be intense enough, and the throat especially quite black. Many black-breasted cocks are white under the throat ; such will never breed nicely marked pullets ; but since black-breasted cocks were demanded for the show-pen, by rigorously refusing all but black-throated birds, and carefully looking for intensity of colour, solidity of hackle, and the other points described above, we have found no difficulty whatever in combining the necessary qualities for producing pullets, with the black breast so coveted for exhibition cocks. It must however be remarked, that while it is easy enough to breed pullets of any colour desired from carefully-bred black breasted cocks, it is very difficult indeed to breed many black-breasted cocks from the beautiful blue-grey birds now so much admired. The cockerels usually produced from even a heavily marked black bird, mated with

such pullets, are mottled-breasted; and these cockerels, bred
from such parentage, make the best birds for pullet-breeding
which can possibly be procured. The very best pullets we
have ever had, have been bred from cockerels produced in
this way.

The brown colour liked by some breeders is little bred now.
Those who still admire it should select a cock with a *few*
brown feathers in the bar of the wing. The breast may be
considerably mottled, and so may the thighs, if the hens be
darkly pencilled on the breast, but the white mottling must
be very sharp and distinct. The stripes in the hackle are
generally rather narrow in this coloured strain; and the tail
may either show green reflections as in that first described,
but darker, or a purple shade. It is also most important to
ascertain that the bird be of a stock breeding the desired
colour; indeed, we should consider this the most important
point of all. Many persons seem to consider that brown
Brahmas must necessarily be crossed. We certainly have
seen some such birds, whose coarse, cruel-looking heads, and
other points, denoted a cross with the Dorking; but many
others present all the characteristics of pure-bred Brahmas,
and in a few years, simply by selection, this colour may be
bred from the purest grey. It is, therefore, more a matter of
fancy than anything else.

In selecting a cock from our own yard for breeding, we
always look first to the wing, then to the saddle and the
tail-coverts, then to the fluff and breast. In purchasing one
from another, we should lay more stress upon the saddle and
coverts, and pay most attention of all to the colour of the

birds he was bred from. With regard to the crossing of different colours, a cock of the dark strain may be mated with hens of either the brown or the silver-grey, and will only darken the pencilling. A cock of the brown strains, mated with hens of the two others, may give pretty tolerable results, giving however brown patches, or stray red feathers, or salmon breasts, to many of the pullets from silver-grey hens. A cock from a light silver-grey yard will breed very few good pullets at all with hens of other colours, unless unusually dark, but will sometimes produce very beautiful and clean-coloured cockerels. A cock from a really good dark blue grey strain will breed well with almost anything. And as the shades of difference are so fine, in claiming a cock at any show, the purchaser should *always* observe carefully the colour of the hens or pullets shown by the same exhibitor, and only complete the transaction if that nearly agrees either with his own, or at least with a permissible cross for the purpose desired.

As in the Light variety, there are many strains of Dark Brahmas in which the silvery white of the upper parts is replaced by a very disagreeable yellow. The fault is hereditary, and of late has been very common, so that even the principal cups of the year have been within our own observation won by cockerels nearly as yellow as a canary. If this tendency be not checked, one of the chief beauties of the fowl will soon be lost. The sun will sometimes cause a yellow tinge even in good white birds, but not if there be plenty of shade ; whereas the hereditary kind of yellow appears when the bird is kept from any sun at all. We believe the tint was originally introduced by a cross with the Cochin, and cannot too strongly express our dislike of it as a most unsightly blemish.

Dark Brahmas have on several occasions been extensively crossed with both Cochins and Grey Dorkings. In the case of Cochins the Partridge variety has been usually employed, and the motive we believe has been either to obtain darker breasted pullets, or to recover cushion and fluff when too much lost from ignorant breeding. The Cochin breast will be one sign of such impurity in the blood, while the expression of the face is often very different from that of pure bred birds. But the best test is the occurrence of red feathers about the hocks or fluff of the cockerels, with yellow in the hackle ; and if in addition the hens bred from the same stock have red about the shoulders, the evidence will be pretty conclusive. Red or brown about a pullet's breast is however no proof whatever of a Cochin cross, as the purest bred birds will occasionally show it.

The Dorking cross has been attempted for several objects. Some have tried the experiment with a view to gain earlier growth, the Dorking being a quickly maturing fowl, while the Brahma grows late. Others have desired to improve the quality of the meat—a legitimate object enough if the parentage were avowed ; whilst some have hoped to improve the pencilling on the breast, always the difficult point with Brahma breeders. Many exhibitors doubt the existence of this cross at all ; and on one occasion, at the Birmingham Show, when we pointed out a prize pen as certainly containing Dorking blood, we were met with an amount of ridicule which we do not wish to encounter again. But facts quite justified our assertion; for in April of the following year we had a letter from a friend who had purchased a nest of eggs from the exhibitor of that very pen, stating that one of the chicks had the well-known *five claws!* As to detection of the cross, white legs are one sign of it. We rarely even yet visit a show without seeing somewhere a white-legged pullet, though they are less common than they were; and we believe this fault to have been introduced entirely by the Dorking cross, except where lime is used in the yard. We have seen birds all but perfect in every other point : and would not condemn such, as a good yellow-legged cock might obviate the fault in her progeny : but unless the bird was reared on a lime bottom it shows that a taint *has* existed, though nearly bred out again. A great want of cushion is another sign of Dorking blood, but is not to be trusted to alone, as bad selection in breeding will produce the same fault. On the whole the best sign is a large, " sour," cruel-looking head, which is generally the last evidence to quit a strain once contaminated, being often present even after the white leg has disappeared. A Brahma pullet may have much too long or too large a head for beauty, and yet be pure, provided the *expression* be gentle and pleasing ; but we would never trust to any strain which bred cruel-looking birds. Minor signs are, too ample tail in the cocks, or too large wings, or comb very high in the centre division and not at the sides, or much white in the tail ; but all these points should be considered and compared in doubtful cases before a decision is pronounced. Even the

white leg, as we have said, we have found can be produced in
a pure strain by allowing the birds to run on lime for a whole
season. For some years the Dorking cross had nearly disappeared, but we have lately seen it again on several occasions.

Passing on now to the practical business of the breeding
yard, we may say a word about selecting eggs. So many
follies have been uttered concerning this matter, that we
almost fear to hazard a fresh assertion. But in our own
experience we have generally found, that the best shaped
Brahma pullets were produced from eggs rather short and
round ; whilst *very* long eggs, especially if much pointed at
the small end, almost always bred pullets with some awk-
wardness in style or carriage, though often first-class cockerels.
It is, however, certain that *smooth-shelled* eggs alone are
proper for hatching in this variety, rough shells generally
showing some derangement of the organs, and being often
broken. The color is of little importance : we prefer a rather
dark egg, but the best hen we ever possessed for breeding
laid eggs perfectly white.

Eggs should be chosen of the fair average size *usually
laid by the hen they are from*, any unusually large or small
being rejected. The absolute size is of little importance, some
hens laying immense eggs, and others very small ones. A fat
hen will always lay small eggs, which can only produce small
and weakly chicks ; but small eggs from a healthy bird often
produce first-class fowls. Over-fattening is the great evil of
our present system of exhibition. We have had eggs sent us
for inspection by indignant purchasers from celebrated ex-

hibitors, little larger than those of a Bantam, and sterile of course. We would not set such if we knew them to be from the very best pen ever seen, and to sell them is a real fraud, though it is often done in ignorance of their worthlessness.

The shells of Brahma eggs are generally unusually thick and dense; and hence in hot weather the chicks are very liable to perish unless the eggs are wetted, or the nest itself be on the ground in a damp place. There is no need of daily sprinkling them as some advocate; but plenty of water will do them good. Our usual plan is to take the hen off at night about a week before hatching, in summer, and empty a good *half-pint* of warm water over the nest and eggs, repeating the operation a second time the third day after, and once more the day before the eggs are to chip, replacing the mother immediately. We never remove the chicks; but as soon as all are hatched the whole family should of course be removed to a dry place.

To secure early eggs from the two-year-old hens is of great importance; and we have found that much can be done towards this by skilful management, always getting eggs from some of our hens early in January. It will be found that hens which have laid late into the season before will not lay till late in the new year; and hence such birds as are valued for next year's breeding should be allowed, as they become broody in the autumn, either to hatch and rear a brood, or to sit on the nest for six weeks. In the latter case they should have more food than is usual with sitting hens, but not enough to cause fattening: and the usual result is to hasten the moult, which the bird then gets through without laying, and will

commence in due time after.   If however, the moult finds a
hen laying, she will very often continue the supply of eggs
till the process is nearly completed, and early eggs cannot
then be expected.   This point is of the more importance,
because the eggs of pullets, which can of course be had in any
quantity, are not so good for early broods ; though we have
reared very fine early birds from the more vigorous of our
young stock.

The sex of Brahma chickens can in nine cases out of ten
be easily distinguished at about a fortnight old.   The wings
of the little cockerels are narrow and pointed, while in the
pullets they are broad and rounded at the end.   The cockerels
also show much dark colour in the wing feathers, while the
pullets are nearly white in the light breed, and pencilled in
the dark.   Later on, pencilling generally appears in the wings
of the cockerels also ; but the difference is still easily seen by
the pullets fledging down the breast and on the shoulders,
long before the cockerels show a vestige of body-feathering
anywhere.   Not unfrequently pullets may be seen almost
fledged, while the cockerels are nearly bare, especially when
the parents on both sides are young birds.

The chicks being hatched, and supposed to be good in
quality, the immediate object is to get them to the greatest
possible size.   With this view many people employ custard :
but we have perfectly satisfied ourselves that, whatever this
mixture of milk and eggs coagulated by heat may do for
Dorking chickens, it is at least thrown away upon Brahmas.
We are not sure that even *better* results cannot be produced
without it ; at all events birds quite as large can be reared

without, and we believe that the best food for this and all
large-boned breeds is coarse oatmeal, mixed with milk and
ground bones, or the "bone-dust" used by gardeners for
potting plants.* The use of this latter substance has many
advantages, and after several years' experience we can affirm
without hesitation that there is a marked difference both
in the size and stamina of birds reared with it over others.
It adds to the size of the birds : it postpones their maturity,
or "setting" as poultry men call it, after which growth nearly
ceases : it greatly prevents leg-weakness in the cockerels ; and
it tends to produce full and profuse feathering, and to assist
in fledging. Burnt bones, or phosphate of lime, have not the
same effect by any means ; and raw bones crushed have the
fault of inducing early laying in the pullets, whereas the bone-
dust rather postpones it. The fœtid odour is of no consequence whatever with chickens, but communicates a most
offensive taste to the eggs of pullets if given after laying has
commenced.

For the young chickens while with the hen there is no
better food than that recommended by our Scotch friend,
which is mixed as follows :—Crumbled bread, one thick slice ;
coarse oatmeal and *grass cut small*, of each a tea-cupful ;
bone-dust one ounce ; mixed with new milk to the proper
crumbly consistence. As they get older the bread may be
somewhat lessened, but some should always be given, as it
makes the mixture take up more milk, which is an object.

* For the knowledge of this ingredient we were first indebted to Mr. John
Stuart, a well-known Scotch fancier, with whom we have exchanged many a long
letter on poultry matters, leading to a friendship which personal acquaintance has
only deepened and improved.

We have also found chickens soon tire of oatmeal alone. For young broods this food should always be mixed crumbly; but when they get about two months old they like it better with rather more milk. When they get tired of the oatmeal, for a change a mixture of equal parts of sharps or middlings and barley meal should be substituted, still adding the bone-dust and a little bread, and mixing with milk so that it will *break* when thrown on the ground. Enough should be given to satisfy the broods without leaving any; and they should be fed as often as any real appetite returns, which will be every two hours when first hatched, but will soon extend to every three hours. To get very large birds this constant care in feeding is absolutely necessary, though good sized fowls may be reared with less.

In addition to the feeding, the chicks should have every morning, the first thing, as much new milk as they will drink, and again some time in the afternoon. They are very fond of it, and it makes a considerable difference in their size, while it assists them wonderfully in early seasons. On cold days a little crushed hemp seed may be added to the food with advantage. We never found our own Brahmas need ale, or that they were any the better for it, but in some cases it might perhaps be given with benefit. The milk should however be left off at about two months old, or in very hot weather.

The last feed at night should always consist of grits, chopped with a knife for the first few days. For a change canary seed may be given, and when older, buckwheat. And a little boiled liver or other cooked meat chopped fine, should be given once, and once only, every day.

Up to the middle of March the broods should have a feed every night at about ten o'clock, dry grits giving the least trouble, with as much as they will drink of warm milk. If the hen and her brood can be brought into the house so much the better. A little patience is often required to teach them to feed at night, and for several times they will often eat little or nothing, or even refuse to come out at all. In such a case we set down the light, lift the hen off the chickens bodily, and scatter the grits among them before she has time to cover them again. She will then call them to the food; and in a few days they learn that candle-light means "grub," and come out to fill their tiny crops with great satisfaction.

Almost the only ailment Brahma chickens are subject to is cramp in the feet. Mere cold is seldom the reason of this, but damp ground will almost always cause it in a portion of every brood till the weather becomes mild, though the offspring of adult birds are less subject to it. The chicks look perfectly well, till some of them are observed with a tendency to close the claws as though roosting, and this increases until the poor little wretch has to walk upon its knuckles in a manner painful to witness. The milk and bone-dust, with meat once a day, will guard against it in a measure; but in bad weather in February or March some cases will be sure to occur, unless the breeder has a shed floored with *perfectly* dry dust or earth, in which case he will not be troubled unless his stock is weakly. Even bad cases, however, can be cured. The treatment is, to provide a cage near enough to the fire to be comfortably warm, well furnished with fine dry ashes, and to remove the chicks to it, only restoring them to the hen when

she is brought in at night. They are to be fed as usual, and
five or six times a day must be taken out and their feet
bathed in warm water, opening out the claws to the natural
position under the water, and keeping them so for about a
minute, when the chick must be put back in the cage. When
it begins to recover, it may now and then be left with the hen
for an hour or two on sunny days, but not in bad weather till
perfectly well. Much patience may be required, and we have
had chicks which needed a fortnight's treatment ere they were
quite restored; but we never had one case we did not conquer
at last, unless the chick had been left for many days before
treatment was commenced.

If the chicks are bred in confinement the supply of green
food must be unlimited ; and the best is grass cut into green
chaff with a pair of scissors, and thrown on the ground by
itself as well as mixed in the meal. They will eat much
more of it this way than if they have to pluck it from a
turf. On a grass run of course this will not be needed.

At ten weeks to three months old the cockerels *must* be
separated from the pullets if fine birds are desired. When kept
together, the pullets lay much sooner, and the cockerels
" furnish " or finish their fledging, and both stop growing.
The cockerels are best turned into a run in company with an
old cock, who will generally keep order, and agree very well
with them until they are first shown ; but after absence at a
show each bird thus removed will have to be provided for
separately, or there will be a fight on return.

The same period is a convenient time for picking out all
evident " wasters," which can generally be known at this age.

Dark pullets must not be discarded for light breasts, as the pencilling often does not develope till the feathers change : but a very streaky bird may be safely condemned, as may any which show great splashes of white or brown about the back and shoulders. Dark cockerels which are nearly white on the breast, of which one or two may occur in the darkest strains at this age, should also be picked out ; but well-shaped and promising chickens should not be rejected for any amount of brown in the wings, as this will often nearly or quite disappear with the adult plumage. It is worth noting, that the general carriage of the cockerels can be judged better at about ten weeks old, than at any subsequent age until the bird assumes his matured appearance.

Light Brahmas at the same period often show a great deal of black, especially on the backs of the pullets and fluff of the cockerels. Sometimes this will remain even until six months old, and still disappear ; so that the fancier should be cautious how he discards promising birds on account of too much black, before they are full grown.

Like all other large fowls, Brahma cockerels are somewhat subject to leg-weakness, caused simply by the growth being more rapid than the constitution can bear. The progeny of young birds are most subject to it ; but the use of bone-dust in the food, as we have recommended, with a little sulphate of iron in the drinking water, we can state from experience is almost a preventive. Since we adopted this system of feeding we have only had one case, and that a very mild one, though we have often bred from young birds ; and we believe if the plan be generally followed it will be almost needless to

prescribe any treatment for this well-known infirmity; but as
the bone-dust is sometimes difficult to procure, we give the
following prescription by Mr. Joseph Hinton :—

Sulphate of Iron	..	1 grain.
,, Strychnia*	...	$\frac{1}{16}$,,
Phosphate of Lime ...	...	5 ,,

to be given three times a day for about six weeks ; but unless
the bird is likely to prove valuable it had better be killed.

There is yet another danger through which the chickens,
especially the cockerels, have to pass before they are ready
for the show-pen. It rarely troubles those who have an
extensive grass run for their birds—happy indeed are such!—
but all who breed in confined space know too well how
surely, in due time, many of their best young cocks acquire
the deformity known in the fancy as a "slipped" or "turned
wing," caused by the flights protruding in disorder outside
the other feathers. If neglected the whole wing often gets
into hopeless confusion, and almost past remedy. There is a
form of disordered wing which is indeed hereditary and
incurable, being caused by the feathers *growing* spiral-fashion,
or twisted on their own axes ; but it is happily very rare.
Whenever this occurs it should be ruthlessly " stamped out ;"
but mere displacement can be cured in most cases if *taken in
time.* It occurs sometimes very early, but usually about four
to five months old, and in confined yards is occasioned by the
bird being driven by others, or otherwise frightened, causing
the wing to be so rapidly extended, that when re-closed the

---

* On account of the danger from an overdose of the strychnia, these pills should
be made up by a chemist, unless the breeder possesses the necessary knowledge.

feathers are not properly returned. Even a single such occurrence will sometimes cause the blemish ; but if not, a few
repeated soon confirm the fault, which greatly mars the beauty
of the bird, and as it arises at an age when the quills are not
hardened, becomes permanent if not cured.

The cure is easy, simple, and very rarely fails—at all
events, while many of our own cockerels, being reared in
very small runs, have been more or less affected, we have
had but few cases which care and patience did not perfectly

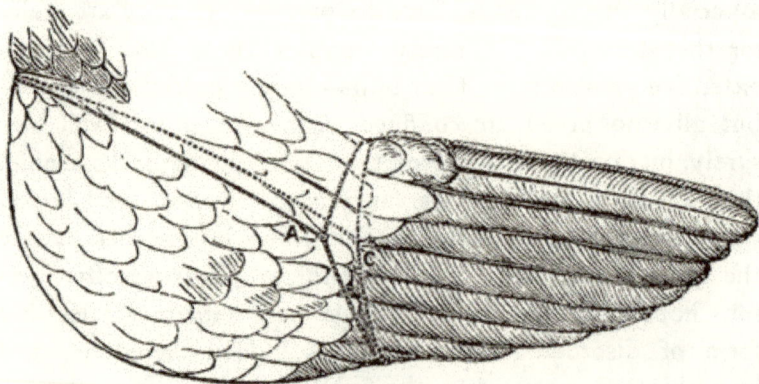

Fig. 9.

subdue. If it occurs early it should be treated at once, but
later on nothing can be done until the chicken-feathers are
cast, and the new or adult quills of the wing are grown long
enough to hold a ligature. This is usually at from eighteen
to twenty-two weeks old ; and as soon as it appears to be the
case, the bird is to be taken by candle-light (for the sake of
quietness) and the wing carefully replaced in the proper
position. Everything depends upon *each feather* being duly
returned ; and this much having been ascertained, the wing

must be bound round rather tightly, as near the shoulder as possible, with soft string about the thickness of whipcord, bringing the knot to about the middle of the outside. The cord must then be passed from the knot round the shoulder or web of the wing, and tied again to the middle of the ligature on the inside ; which will effectually prevent the bird slipping off the unwelcome restraint, as he will endeavour to do. Fig. 9 will explain what is meant to the merest tyro. The beginner may occasionally find he has made either the ligature or the retaining cord too slack ; in which case he will next morning find the bird has again slipped the flights out of place, and the work must be done over again the following night. If on the other hand the shoulder or retaining cord be drawn too tight, it will cut and become embedded in the web of the wing, causing the bird much pain and distress. After one or two trials the proper tension of both cords will be ascertained, and no further difficulty found. Most birds will submit to the operation quietly enough if taken from their perch, but even when restive patience and tact will always prevail. Some wings are particularly awkward to tie, and we remember one fine cockerel in particular, whose wing we had to tie up afresh every night for a whole week, before all the feathers were retained in place to our satisfaction ; but we effected it at last, and eventually sold him for a large sum, perfectly cured.

The bird must be kept with his wing or wings tied up for at least three weeks, or until the quills appear grown their full length, when the ligature may be cut. The chances are that one wing may now appear cured, and the

other not ; and if either or both are still in fault, the operation must be patiently repeated. We have had birds that
occasioned us more than two months of watchful care ; but
excepting in those whose treatment had been delayed rather
too long, scarcely ever had a case yet we did not overcome in
the end.

Pullets are subject to the same fault, but not nearly so
often as the cockerels ; and even adult birds will sometimes
require attention to their wings during moulting time. Where
the tendency is slight, it is often sufficient simply to see the
wing is properly tucked up every night at roost during the
critical period. We do not think we ever knew a bad case
where the birds had the run of a large grass field, unless
there was a strong hereditary tendency to it.

With the approach of warm weather it is best to discontinue
giving any meat to the chickens, or the combs of the young
cocks will have a tendency to grow too large, and the pullets
would lay too early for large size. Indeed, it is very difficult
in fine seasons to prevent early pullets from laying at about
five months old, as they reach that age at a time of year
when everything favors the production of eggs ; but where
there is room much can be done by constant watchfulness and
attention, and the eventual size will greatly depend upon the
success with which the tendency can be warded off. Milk
and all stimulating food should therefore be discontinued, but
the bone-dust should still be given, having a decided tendency
to keep the birds raw or unformed. As the combs develope
and become red the pullets should be carefully watched, and
as soon as there seems the slightest reason to suspect the

approach of laying, be removed to a strange run. This will usually check the production of eggs for a fortnight at least, and the same expedient may often be employed for a second time with success, but rarely more than this if the bird has been really on the point of laying. It is better, therefore, when possible, to move each lot of pullets to a strange run every three weeks or so from the time they are four months old, by which even early birds may often be kept from laying till after seven months, to their great advantage. To attempt postponing laying longer than this rarely answers, often producing an undesirable moult just when the pullet is wanted for show.

We never like to see a young cock look "pretty" at too early an age : such a bird may win at a very early show, but by Christmas will appear a dwarf. Neither are we pleased to see three-months chickens of either sex too short on the leg : such also rarely make fine birds. It is the business of chicks to make *frame*, on which flesh and feathers will soon come after; and it is the raw, ugly-looking, long-legged birds, whose hackle is long in coming, and whose wattles show but little, which in the end make giants for the show-pen. Even at six months old the best cockerels generally appear very raw and unformed, with hackle not half grown, and a length of leg no one could believe would ever seem less; but two months more will tell a different tale, and produce magnificent birds, beside which the precocious ones of September are not fit to stand.

Cockerels should therefore be hatched early, and in our opinion are at their best when eight or nine months old ; but a few months more does them little injury provided the upper plumage remain a good white, which in confinement is often not the case. Pullets, on the contrary, are often hatched too soon, and by the time they have to be shown at Birmingham have got long past their best condition, having reduced themselves by laying. When this has once commenced there is nothing like a grass run to keep them fresh; but we think they never look quite so well as while laying their first few eggs. Pullets intended for Birmingham are therefore better hatched towards the end of April; and though cockerels of the same date are often scarcely mature enough, they usually make larger birds eventually than if hatched at either a later or earlier period.

We are convinced that Brahma chickens can be reared to the best advantage of all, in grass yards of only moderate size; say about one thousand square feet, which will rear a dozen fine cockerels and remain green. With unlimited range the birds cannot be got to feed so regularly; and though in beautiful condition, mature too soon to make large fowls. On the other hand, cockerels bred in confinement seldom take enough exercise; and hence, though easily reared to a great size, often acquire an ungainly carriage which birds with more liberty never have.

With regard to actual show condition, however, we are more and more convinced that nothing can equal the effect of a good wide grass run, with plenty of shrubbery to give shade. Birds thus happily situated will only need to have as much soft food as they will eat for three weeks before any show, and to have their legs and feet washed the night before sending off; unless they appear wild, when they should be accustomed to being penned. This is easiest accomplished by putting them in a pen every night for a week, and keeping them confined till about an hour after they have been fed in the morning, when they should not be taken out, but allowed to come quietly of themselves. If they are too thin they may be kept up in a dry shed for a fortnight, letting them out on the grass for an hour daily to keep up the appetite and give them exercise.

In exhibiting Brahmas bred in confinement, the difficulty is to obtain gloss and hardness of plumage ; but even in such circumstances much can be done by attention and care. The most scrupulous cleanliness must be observed both in house and run ; and as before recommended, a shed floored with *perfectly* dry material is of the utmost importance. If any washing be needed, it should be done a few days before the show, in order that there may be time for a fresh secretion of oil to restore the gloss. Till the bird is thoroughly dry it should be kept in a dry room with nothing but straw or chaff on the floor, lest it should soil the washed plumage while damp : but when dry it may be returned to the shed, into which should be tipped some bushels of finely cut straw, enough to cover the earth or ashes all over several inches deep. This will keep the plumage perfectly clean and nice (at least so far as anything can), and the birds enjoy it greatly.

The parts most likely to need washing in Dark Brahmas are the wings of the cocks and cushion of the pullets. Many pullets appear brown on the cushion from no other reason than that they were reared in small runs, the earth in which they dust themselves adhering to a certain extent to the

plumage of this part, which is not so close as on the rest of
the body. We hardly know whether to recommend washing
or not: much depending on the skill with which it is done, and
the time allowed to recover. The final rinsing should be done
with water slightly blued, but not so much so as to give the
effect of a dye—just as much as will still allow a white bird to
appear white. It is very difficult for any but a professed
"poultry-man" in constant practice to wash a fowl well; and
if only moderately clean we should advise an inexperienced
amateur to let his birds go as they are. The straw chaff
mentioned will clean them to a great extent, and improve
their health at the same time.

With regard to feeding in confinement, the great thing is to
give the birds as much as they will eat with healthy appetite
and no more. Were the condition in which Game fowls are
shown more favoured by exhibitors and judges, breeders in
towns would be more on a level with their country brethren ;
but to obtain hardness of feather with the *weight* necessary
to win, is not an easy matter in a small yard. Peas, to which
the Game cock owes so much, would give hardness to the
Brahma, but will not make size and weight. On the whole
we consider the best feeding for grown chickens to be a good
feed of any meal morning and noon, with grain at night,
adding some linseed stewed into a jelly to the soft food every
third day during the last fortnight. If the birds are not *over-*
fed this will do no harm, and gives much gloss to the feather.
The cockerels may with great advantage for a month previous,
have daily some fresh or *raw* bones, crushed as recommended
by Mr. Crook, to the size of peas ; but for the pullets it would

be too stimulating to give this, for fear of hypertrophy of the egg organs. The effect of it is considerable in giving condition to the young cocks, but they are apt to become very combative in a small yard.

. The use of sulphate of iron in the water will bring out the bright red colour of the combs and wattles; and before sending off, these parts of town-bred birds should be well washed—for which purpose a common nail-brush is very handy—and then carefully sponged with vinegar, taking care, however, not to injure the eyes. Any *stray* broken or foul feather may be plucked out without wrong, and finally a careful smoothing over with a silk handkerchief will do about all that can be honestly done for the birds. The rest must be left for the judges.

If the journey to the show be a long one, there is no better expedient for refreshing the birds on the way than that recommended by Mr. Wragg* of tying half a loaf inside the hamper on one side, and a fresh cabbage on the other. They should in such circumstances be sent off by the night *mail trains*, which will reach almost any place by good time in the morning, and the birds miss their food but little. Should they appear overdone, if the owner is with them, a table-spoonful of port wine will often make a wonderful difference.

We only make one final remark. Brahmas will not bear *continual* showing. Could they be shown with success in the state Game fowls are—and we take this last opportunity of expressing, however hopelessly, our emphatic opinion that

---

* Practical Poultry Keeper, page 93.

this is the condition in which *all* fowls ought to be shown—
no breed would surpass them in endurance of fatigue ; but to
carry the weight of flesh and fat success demands, with the
excitement and confinement of exhibition added, breaks them
down sooner than Cochins, on account of their naturally
active disposition.   We have repeatedly known celebrated
cup cockerels purchased at as much as £20, which proved
perfectly sterile, having been ruined and broken down in
constitution by over-exhibition ; and there is no judge but has
repeatedly to express his regret at seeing some noble cock,
winner perhaps only the week before, either actually para-
lysed in the legs or too weak to stand in his pen.   To show
birds thus is to display the *vices* of the poultry fancy—to
carry to sinful excess in rivalry one of the most healthful,
innocent, and useful pursuits open as recreation for the
wearied body and mind of man ; and whenever we come
across such a case, we feel it hard to conceal our contempt for
the gambling spirit which can gorge and then wear out a poor
bird, just for the sake of one more prize.

CHAPTER V.

On the Judging of Brahmas.

THE mistake an inexperienced judge is most likely to fall into in deciding the merits of the pens in a Brahma class, is to confound the type with that of the Cochin, from which, as we have seen, it is quite distinct in various respects. So great, in fact, is this danger, that it may be well again to point out in brief the differences between the two races.

While the tail of the Cochin, then, should be as small, low, and soft as possible, that of the Brahma should be nearly upright, of a tolerable size, containing some amount of quill, and the top feathers if possible spreading out as before described. The Cochin plumage is of a loose or downy character, while the Brahma is a hard-feathered breed, or should be when shown in proper "condition;" hence the Brahma, though fully furnished, has less fluff than the Cochin, and the hen is rather square than "lumpy" in shape. The Cochin is quiet and solid : the Brahma *should* be sprightly and active. The breast of a Brahma should be deep and full, with the crop low down. Again, while the cushion of a Cochin hen is almost globular in form, burying the tail, that of a Brahma should rise more and more in a slightly *hollow* curve, till it merges into the nearly upright tail. And finally, the peculiar head—exactly resembling that of a grouse—though it cannot always be seen in perfection, will always receive some attention from a good judge.

With regard to a "scale of points" for judging, Mr. Tegetmeier was unquestionably the first to conceive the idea, which in our opinion was of great value, though his scale has long since ceased to be of practical use, owing partly no doubt to the very limited competition at the time it was framed. Mr. Tegetmeier's scale was as follows :—

POINTS OF BRAHMAS.

Size	3
Color	4
Head and Comb	1
Wings. Primaries well tucked under secondaries	1
Legs, and feathering of ditto	1
Fluff	1
Symmetry	2
Condition	2
Total	15

DISQUALIFICATIONS. - Birds not matching in the pen ; combs not uniform in the pen, or falling over to one side ; crooked backs ; legs not feathered to the toes, or of any color except yellow or dusky yellow.

The system implied here is easily understood. A pullet perfect in color will count 4 on that ground ; but if not perfect will count only 3, 2, or 1, according to the judge's opinion of her marking; or if he thinks her very bad will lose 4 points. If wanting in leg-feather, however, she will only lose 1. Thus all her points are added up, and by the result she is to be compared with other birds. If, however, a bird has a bad falling comb, it is to be disqualified; and the same of a crooked back and some other faults.

K

Now applying this to the decisions of the best judges, it will be found, that while often pretty consistent, many evidently *correct* decisions do not harmonise with it. For instance, let us suppose a cockerel to lose one point by not being very large, another by a little want of condition, and another by some degree of fault in the comb : if perfect in other matters his numerical value would be 12. The bird in the next pen might carry every point with the sole exception of symmetry, in which he was very greatly wanting, being clumsy in shape and most ungainly in carriage : this fault would lose him 2 points, and his value would be 13, beating the other by one point. But we have not the least hesitation in saying that nearly any judge—certainly any *good* judge— would exactly reverse such a conclusion. Many other similar cases might be given, and are constantly occurring.

After many trials to amend it, we felt persuaded that 15 points were *not sufficient* to form any reliable "standard" at all of some breeds ; and that there were several elements unmentioned, which ought to be included in the calculation. Respecting some points, also, opinion has perceptibly changed since Mr. Tegetmeier's scale was published. We therefore in the first two editions of this work suggested an extended scale, not as our own opinion merely, but as embodying what careful comparison taught us was the value *practically* given to various points, as evidenced by the best actual *decisions* of Messrs. Hewitt and Teebay during the previous four years. This amended table of values stood as follows ; the italics representing our own personal views only, and all the rest being deduced from actual analysis ; decisions apparently erroneous having been excluded from the computation. We soon found it needful to separate the sexes.

THE COCK.

POINTS OF MERIT.		SPECIAL DEFECTS.	
Size	4	*To count against the bird in proportion to their degree.*	
Color	4		
Smallness, shape, and expression of Head	1	Stain of white in deaf-ear	1
Comb	2	White legs*	3
Fullness of Hackle	1	Primaries of wing not tucked in	3
Wings, proper size and position of	1	*Vulture hocks*	3 to 4
Legs and feathering	2	*White in the tail*	3
Fluff	1		
Breadth of Saddle	1	DISQUALIFICATIONS.	
Rise of ditto	1	Round or crooked back, crooked	
Tail	2	beak, or any bodily deformity;	
Symmetry	2	knock-knees, or any fraudulent	
Condition and handsome appearance	3	dressing or trimming.	
	25		

With reference to the table of defects, it should be observed that manifestly only those can be inserted which are not provided for in the points of merit. Thus, smallness would be a great fault ; but the bird would according to the points of merit lose four by want of size, and no other provision is therefore necessary. So of defects in comb and feathering. The table of defects is only needed for special faults which in practice are found not sufficiently accounted for in the general scale.

---

* A white or pinky-legged bird to be disqualified, unless very perfect in other respects.

Our table for the Hen stood as follows :—

POINTS OF MERIT.	
Size - -	3
Beauty and regularity of color and marking -	4
Smallness and beauty of head -	2
Comb -	1
Shortness and breadth of back	1
Cushion - - -	2
Fluff -	1
Legs and feathering -	2
Shape - - -	2
Condition, carriage, and general appearance - -	2
	—
	20

SPECIAL DEFECTS.	
White legs	2
Very long tail	2
Primaries not tucked in	3
Very streaky feathers, though otherwise good color (in Dark)	2
Shank feathering not pencilled as body (in Dark)	1
Spotted back (in Light)	2
Vulture hocks -	2 to 3

DISQUALIFICATIONS.

Rough or crooked backs; crooked bills; knock-knees, or any bodily deformity; large red or white splashes in the Dark breed ; pinky legs, or any fraudulent dyeing, dressing or trimming.

In the hen, it will be observed, we attached more value to the head and less to the comb than in the cock. This is in conformity both with all recent decisions, and with strict propriety ; as are the other variations from or additions to the numerical values given for the male bird.

The scales thus given were found to represent very correctly modern judging, so far as such a limited number of points could do so; but on the publication of the American "Standard of Excellence," soon after the second edition of this work was issued, we became at once convinced of the infinite superiority of a scale of 100 points, as giving room for *gradation* in deducting values. The American scale for Brahmas followed our scale for the hen *almost exactly*, only modifying it as

regards head and comb by our scale for the cock: and as
the scale for this breed was adopted after a longer and more
searching discussion than was bestowed upon any other, this
result furnished a most gratifying testimony to the general
accuracy of our calculations. This American scale stood as
follows :—

AMERICAN SCALE OF "POINTS IN BRAHMAS."

Size	15
Head and Wattles	5
Comb	10
Wings—primaries well tucked under secondaries	10
Legs, Colour and Feathering of	5
Fluff	5
Tail, Form and Carriage of	5
Colour	20
Symmetry	15
Condition	10
	100

This scale will judge Brahmas with very great accuracy;
but it still omits to provide for the difference in values of the
two sexes; and we have ultimately become convinced that for
simplicity of application, accuracy, and comprehensiveness,
the best system by far is to attach values to *defects* only,
rather than to points of merit.   Greater accuracy is thus
secured, because it is no longer needed to keep the sum total
of defects exactly within the 100 points, since some defects
contradict or are inconsistent with others; and we have only
therefore to calculate by analysis of what are considered

correct awards, the exact proportionate value to the 100
points of *each single defect*, regardless of the sum total.   Thus
remodelled, we are able to include both sexes, and both
varieties of Brahmas in one common table of defects, which
are supposed to be deducted from a total of 100 points, taken
as the value of an ideally " perfect" · bird.

In applying such a scale of points as is here given, it
will readily be understood, that the total value of defects
is not to be deducted for every degree of fault in those
particular points.   Neither do they represent the greatest
possible degree of fault, which in many cases would amount
to practical disqualification.   Each value represents as great
a degree of fault as can exist *without* practically debarring
a bird from competition, and the judge will allot such
a proportionate number of points as he considers the
fair proportionate value of the *actual* amount of defect.
Hence " judging by scale" is not so simple as many suppose,
but leaves as much as ever to the appreciation of the actual
judge.   It is not pretended or even wished that birds should
be judged "scale in hand :" such tables as are here given
are more to be studied *at leisure* in order to form the
judgment, or to estimate the chances of any given bird in
competition.   So used they may be of great value ; used
slavishly in the actual judging of large classes (and in
America judges *have* been required to fill up an actual
"scale of points" furnished in blank for every pen) they
will be found an intolerable nuisance to all concerned.

The following, then, is the scale of points now employed
by us ; and, having thoroughly tested it on many occasions,

we can unhesitatingly speak as to its accuracy and ease of application.

VALUE OF DEFECTS IN JUDGING.

To be Deducted fom 100 *Points.*

Bad head and comb (comb to count 7 in cocks, and 5 in hens)	12
Scanty hackle	5
Want of cushion	7
,,　　fluff	6
,,　　leg-feather	7
Vulture hocks	20
Bad shape or carriage of tail	6
White in tail	10
Primaries out of order*	15
Pale legs	8
Curved toes	7
Stain of white in deaf-ear	5
Splashed or streaky breasts in Dark, or black specks in Light	12
Shank-feather (in Dark hens) not pencilled as the body	4
Other faults of colour	10
Want of size	20
,,　general symmetry	15
,,　condition	12
,,　　,,　(if total)	35

DISQUALIFICATIONS.—Birds not tolerably matched. Primary feathers twisted on their axes. Utter absence of leg-feather. Pinky legs. Large red or white splashes in Dark birds, or conspicuous black spots in Light. Round or crooked backs, wry-tails, crooked bills, knock-knees, or any other bodily deformity. Any fraudulent dyeing, dressing, or trimming.

---

* This refers to primaries merely "slipped" outside the wing. For primaries actually twisted on their axes, see list of disqualifications.

It will be found in practice, that a bird which retains after all deductions a value of 86 points, has a very fair chance of first prize ; while 90 points will make winning almost certain, except in *very* severe competition, such as that at Birmingham in 1872, when about one hundred cockerels contended for the honors. About 80 points will often secure second or third prize in very good classes.

For an *unusually* large bird 5 points must be *added* to ensure accuracy. It may seem absurd to some, to add to an " ideal ;" but it will readily be seen on reflection, that there is a fair average size which entitles a bird to be called " perfect," while yet greater size, so far as it goes, ought to count in its favour.

J. WRIGHT AND CO., PRINTERS, STEPHEN STREET, BRISTOL.